RAMSEY
REMEMBERED

RAMSEY
REMEMBERED

The Durham Years

Edited by
Rosalind Brown

Published by Durham Cathedral
www.durhamcathedral.co.uk

Introduction copyright © Rosalind Brown, 2010
Individual contributions and photographs copyright © the
contributors.

First published 2010

Cover design by Hiltonian Media
www.hiltonian.com

ISBN 978-1-90-798100-5

Michael Ramsey in Prior's Hall, Durham Cathedral
(Photo courtesy of the Rt Revd David Stancliffe)

Introduction

Mention Michael Ramsey's name in Durham and someone will tell you a story about him. He is still remembered here with immense affection and some pride. These stories are part of the oral history of Durham and it occurred to me that, unless they are written down, over years to come they will be lost to posterity. So when the suggestion was made by the Rt Revd Stephen Conway, while he was Archdeacon of Durham, that a stained glass window might be commissioned in Michael Ramsey's memory, and the Friends of Durham Cathedral offered to donate it to mark their 75th anniversary, it seemed a good time to collect these stories and publish them as an affectionate tribute to a great man of Durham.

I let it be known that I was looking for stories, especially Durham stories, and they started to come in from people who had known him well and people who had met him only once but still retained the memory of that encounter. The variety of stories was part of the delight of the project; I never knew when I opened a letter or an e-mail whether I would be reading a story that was funny, poignant or profound. Many people wrote a note to tell me how much pleasure it has given them to recall and write down their stories, or to go into attics to dig around original documents. Complete strangers sent me precious original letters for me to look at and copy, as well as photos and newspaper cuttings.

I soon abandoned any idea of grouping the stories according to the period of his life in Durham, or indeed limiting them to Durham stories although the majority fall into that category, and just added them to the file as they arrived. Somehow the lack of arrangement of the stories adds to the sense of discovery as they are read, tumbling out in no particular order just as I experienced them when opening my post. I have not edited out duplicates of the same story—very few are repeated and those that are told more than once are told in different ways by different people—and I have let them stand in the contributor's own words rather than editing them.

I never met Michael or Joan Ramsey, but I feel I have got to know them through this project. I've learned to recognise the hallmarks of a Ramsey story—his repeating of words and his accident-proneness, sometimes perhaps more calculatingly bumbling than people realised—and have marvelled at the number of vivid ways people can describe his walk or the movement of his eyebrows. It seems that he was well aware of the latter since a colleague pointed out this story from Stephen Fry's book, 'Moab is my Washpot'.

'Michael Ramsey, Archbishop of Canterbury during my childhood and during my religious phase a hero and profound influence, was once accused by an interviewer of being wise.

"Am I?" he asked. "I don't think so really, I think it is probably just the impression given by the absurd fecundity of my eyebrows."

"Well, your grace," the interviewer persisted, "how would you define wisdom?"

"Wisdom?" Ramsey chewed the word around in his mouth. "Oh, I should say that wisdom is the ability to cope."' (*Stephen Fry,* Moab is my Washpot. *Arrow Books, 2004, page 238.*)

The stories are still coming in even as I write this and try to bring the search to a close. My thanks are due to colleagues in Durham Cathedral Chapter Office—Diane McIlroy, Dale Robinson, Carol Ross and Eleanor Lancelot—who have typed some of the stories for me over the last year; to Diane McIlroy and Ruth Robson for their help with arranging everything for publication; and to Richard Hilton for the cover design. It goes without saying that I want to thank all the contributors and especially Dr Dai Morgan (who bought 50 South Street from the Ramseys) who kindly let me wander all over his home with a camera. The copyright of the stories remains with the contributors.

I hope that this book brings as much pleasure to people who read it as it has given me when compiling it. It is not a biography but a book to be dipped into to encounter, time and again, a wise man who was one of Durham's great citizens, who inspired affection, caused much mirth, appeared at times to be literally 'lost in wonder, love and praise' and, perhaps above all, left his mark for good on people's lives whether as a result of a brief encounter, a long conversation or something said in a sermon or lecture.

At Durham Cathedral we are delighted to be installing a stained glass window given by the Friends of Durham Cathedral in honour and memory of Michael Ramsey. The 'Transfiguration Window' has been designed by artist Tom Denny, and installed by him and his assistant Michael Lassen. This book is a different kind of tribute to Michael Ramsey from a Cathedral and a city that he loved.

The Revd Canon Rosalind Brown
Canon Librarian, Durham Cathedral, September 2010

Michael and Joan Ramsey in Durham
A very brief chronology

1904:   Michael Ramsey born on 14th November in Cambridge.

1928:   Ordained Deacon.

1929:   Ordained Priest.

1940:   Appointed Canon Professor—Residentiary Canon at Durham Cathedral and Van Mildert Professor of Divinity at Durham University. Lived at 12 The College for most of the time.

1942:   Married Joan Hamilton, then living at 15 The College.

1950:   Left Durham to move to Cambridge (Regius Professor of Divinity) with a subsequent appointment to Lincoln Cathedral.

1952:   Appointed Bishop of Durham. Moved to Auckland Castle, Bishop Auckland.

1956:   Left Durham to move to York (Archbishop of York), and subsequently (1961) Canterbury (Archbishop of Canterbury), then retirement to Cuddesdon in 1974.

1977:   Moved to 50 South Street, Durham.

1978:   Moved to 16 South Bailey, Durham.

1986:   Left Durham to move to Bishopthorpe, York and subsequently to Oxford.

1988:   Michael Ramsey died on 23rd April in Oxford.

1995:   Joan Ramsey died on 13th February in Oxford.

Biographies of Michael Ramsey

Owen Chadwick, *Michael Ramsey: A Life*. Oxford University Press 1990

Michael de-la-Noy, *Michael Ramsey, A Portrait*. William Collins Sons and Co, 1990

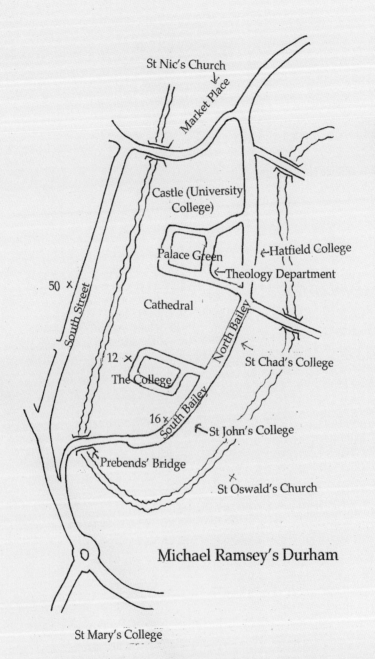

St Nic's Church

Market Place

Castle (University College)

Palace Green

←Hatfield College

←Theology Department

50 ×

South Street

Cathedral

North Bailey

St Chad's College

12 ×

The College

South Bailey

16 ×

↖St John's College

↖Prebends' Bridge

×
St Oswald's Church

Michael Ramsey's Durham

St Mary's College

Ramsey Remembered
The stories from Durham

Michael Ramsey was a good friend of the student Christian movement in Durham and if you needed a preacher which would fill St Mary the Bow, it was Michael Ramsey who would fill it and not Alan Richardson. He was a great favourite. He was very interested in the affairs of the SCM *[Student Christian Movement—Editor]* and I remember meeting him at the bookshop in the town one morning after the very modernist headmaster of Durham School had spoken to the SCM. "Yes, yes, yes and what heresy now? What heresy now?"

There was an occasion one Trinity Sunday when Dean Alington, who was also a very liberal modernist, had taken it into his head to preach about the Athanasian Creed which he didn't really approve of at all; in fact he said it was rubbish. The next Sunday Michael Ramsey also preached on the Athanasian Creed and said, "The Athanasian Creed is very good, very good, very good indeed." He was quite a character in Durham at the time. If you saw him in the pulpit he normally had a pack of papers which hardly had any words on each piece of paper and would deliberately pick the paper up and then drop it down upside down on the pulpit in a very deliberate way, probably twelve pieces of paper but all very brilliant. I remember we had a mission in Durham on the racecourse and Michael Ramsey was chosen as the Mission Preacher and was absolutely brilliant, as you might expect.

He lectured me on gospels and doctrine. We were at St John's which was an evangelical college but we didn't take any notice of the delicacies of the Principal; the great man on whom you depended was Michael Ramsey and he told us to read 'The Ministerial Priesthood' which the Principal of St John's wouldn't allow to be put into the library. We all grew up Anglo-Catholic in doctrine and evangelical in practice.

There are various apocryphal stories which about him of how he managed to go into Masses without his trousers, but I don't know if this was actually true or just a story. He was frequently seen walking around Durham, always on his own of course, walking at great speed with his trousers at half mast. But that was Michael Ramsey. *(The Venerable Leslie Stanbridge)*

During the war years we Choristers saw Canon Ramsey as a gift for those of us who were natural mimics; he was tall, (large when robed), looked elderly even then, had a seafarer's rolling gait as he proceeded through The College, arms folded across his chest, sometimes wearing odd socks, often with a far-away look, but with twinkling, kindly eyes. We enjoyed his Christmas parties.

Later, as Old Choristers, we wrote to congratulate him on his translation to the Archbishopric of York, but, rather mischievously, reminded him that he said that he would never leave Durham. Our Secretary, Revd Peter Welby, received a reply: "Put not your trust in Princes!"

Peter's father, who was Vicar of Bearpark, County Durham, was a great friend and used to walk to see Michael Ramsey almost every morning, accompanied by his dog which he then secured by tying its lead to the Sanctuary Knocker!

I nearly ended his (Ramsey's) distinguished career at Cambridge when he absent mindedly stepped off the pavement; (he was then Regius Professor); his cassock was entangled with the front wheel of my bicycle which fortunately cushioned the impact. He was very decent about it and remembered me as a Durham Old Chorister. *(Alan Oyston)*

After the dedication by Lord Ramsey of the window 'The Last Supper' someone asked him what he thought of it. He clasped his hands behind his back in his usual manner and said, "Well, well" and walked away.

When he was Bishop of Durham he visited clergy in their own homes. On one occasion the visit was to Revd Gordon Defty, Vicar of a large parish in Hartlepool where he had been invited to lunch with Gordon and his curates. The order prior to the lunch from Gordon to his curates was to, "keep the conversation flowing." If conversation were to dry up the signal would be a kick from Gordon directed at one of his curates. Inevitably the one who mistakenly received the kick was the Bishop who thought this very amusing and roared with laughter saying, "I got the kick." This story was told to me by Revd Patrick Kent who is now residing at Sherburn House, County Durham.

After leaving their home in South Street, Bishop Ramsey and his wife moved to accommodation in the South Bailey. During the winter months he used the Cathedral as his daily 'exercise ground'. He would walk round the nave a number of times, his arms behind his back and always in deep contemplation.

The following story again reflects his strong sense of humour and was told to me by the late Mary Adamson, wife of the Headmaster of Bow School. Mary was giving them both a lift in her car when they were involved in a minor accident on the Leazes Bowl roundabout. His comment to friends after the event was an amusing, "And do you know we hit a police car," said with eyes twinkling and eye brows twitching. (*Reg Wright, second Verger, Durham Cathedral, 1975—95*)

My chief memory of Michael Ramsey is of the Founders and Benefactors' Service, which in those days was held on a Wednesday. It always seemed to be rather dark and cold, year by year. Because my name begins with 'W' I was normally at the back of the Senate procession, with AMR [*Arthur Michael Ramsey—Editor*] at the front of the honorary professors, just behind. So it fell out that we often found ourselves sitting next to each other.

On these occasions he would wear a suit, OVER WHICH he wore a dark blue mackintosh, OVER WHICH he wore a red cassock, OVER WHICH he wore an academic gown. He was a big man anyway, and sitting next to him one was squeezed by this vast bundle of layers of clothes. Then at some point in the service a voice would say, "During the singing of the next hymn there will be a collection." At that moment the figure next to me would give a little start, as if this was an entirely new thought; and he would start burrowing through layer after layer, trying to get to his trouser pocket. After much pushing and boring, he would finally get to something, usually just in time; but it made singing the hymn, for those around him, virtually impossible. *(Professor J.R. (Dick) Watson)*

We knew Michael and Joan Ramsey (and their rather fey housekeeper Audrey) during the time they lived in South Bailey. They had previously lived in South Street, which would have been a bit daunting, given the hilly terrain of Durham. Michael had enormous presence: he was a procession in himself, quite capable of stopping traffic as he walked in the middle of the street, and being totally unaware of any problem. He may have been returning to South Street from the Cathedral one day, gently walking uphill from the river. "Is that the Dean and Chapter?" my small son asked. One knew exactly what he meant.

Later on, he would take his daily constitutional round the Cloisters—a prescribed number of circuits, no doubt. I never saw him and Joan walking together, but they would have made a contrasting pair. Joan had an inner ear problem, and did not necessarily walk in straight lines. Michael, on the other hand, was like a steam ship, with her as a sailing boat beside him.

Their chapel was absolutely beautiful, decorated with works of art— presents from around the world: a room one would want to spend time in, though I am not sure how tranquil it was, being on the street-side of the house.

Joan and Michael were very sweet together: she did not take him altogether seriously. One day he had spots of ink on his hand: "He thinks he has blue blood", said Joan, smilingly. We were invited to drinks on an ordinary day, just us. Michael wore his patent leather shoes, with silver buckles. *(Katherine Venning)*

I heard that one Ash Wednesday, Michael preached at a service in St John's College. Afterwards, when he was given a drink in the SCR [*Senior Common Room—Editor*], a pert student asked him whether he did not think it wrong to drink sherry now that Lent had started. The eyebrows twitched. "I regard it as a mortification", he replied. *(Mark Venning)*

As an 'Aidan's Maiden' from 1950—54, I value enormously Bishop Michael Ramsey's ministry, whether in sermons, lectures or debates, or in his writings, such as his book about prayer, 'Be still and know' (1982).

It was a joy to see him escorting the Queen at her coronation in 1953, looking, as always, like a benevolent grandfather!—it seemed so 'right' for him to be beside this young woman as she undertook so awesome a responsibility.

At the time when Miss EM Scott, the first Principal of St Aidan's Society (as it still was in my day) died, Archbishop Ramsey had retired back to Durham. There was a memorial service for her attended by many of her former students, and we were very touched that he joined us in the congregation, wearing simply his black cassock, and we remembered with gratitude that he had been as passionate about higher education for women as Miss Scott was. *Deo Gloria!*

On another later Reunion weekend, I attended that Sunday morning service in the Cathedral instead of at St Nic's, and it happened that Bishop Ramsey was the preacher. On the way out, I was delighted to hear two gentlemen, clearly visitors, remark, smiling, to each other: "Hmm! He preached the gospel, which is what one expects a father in God to do!" Amen to that. *(Margaret C. Calow)*

When the Ramseys retired, there was a small kerb a few feet from the front door over which Michael fell, followed by Joan who fell on top of him. "Goodness", I said, "Whatever happened next?" "We were a most terrible writhing heap, writhing heap, writhing heap, until Miss Etchells (Principal of St John's) arrived and offered us a warm drink. Oh dear, we'd so much rather have had a glass of whisky!"

The best story Colin Slee and I collected was that our Archbishop, Michael Ramsey, visited a Fr Whitehead in California (he would also travel whenever possible via California so that he could visit him again), went for a walk in old borrowed mac and got lost. A young man picked him up, asking if he was lost—"Yes, I am lost"—and eventually took him back to Fr Whitehead. Next year, on arriving, he asked how that boy was. "Oh, he's in hospital." "I caused a car to be brought and take me to the hospital. There I was in my purple cassock. I was taken to the ward by a nice sister and as she was about to draw back the curtains, asked who I was. 'The Archbishop of Canterbury', I said. She drew back the curtains and announced, 'The Archbishop of Canterbury to see you.' To which the young man replied, 'Oh God, not again!'"

The Dean of Southwark and I think this quite the most wonderful story from the cornucopia of fun. *(The Very Revd Victor Stock)*

Geoffrey Fisher *[Archbishop of Canterbury before Michael Ramsey, and his former Headmaster—Editor]* never quite digested the fact that a pupil of his from Repton was (already) Archbishop of Canterbury and his direct and immediate successor. Fisher kept writing to Ramsey, at least twice a week and on occasion to The Times. Ramsey became more and more depressed by this avalanche of unwanted and unhelpful advice and criticism. His staff noticed, Joan noticed. He stopped humming and talking to himself. Then there was a particular attack and Ramsey went off one morning all alone in his Morris Minor. Everyone slowly realised that no one knew where he had gone, not secretary, nor office staff, nor chaplain, nor Joan. They were anxious. He returned at lunch time, parked in front of the steps, they rushed out to meet him, smiling, humming, singing to himself. As they ascended the stairs the chaplain, behind them, ventured, "Your Grace, may we be permitted to know where you have been?" "Yes, yes, yes. I've been to Madame Tussaud's. I've been to Madame Tussaud's, to be measured, measured. And they're melting down Geoffrey Fisher."

On one occasion, after retirement Edith was having coffee with him in Holy Week on the lawn of the Master's Lodge at Corpus Cambridge. "If anything you seem busier since retiring than before." She said. "Ah yes, ah yes, but NOW I can be selective." *(The Very Revd Colin Slee)*

Michael Ramsey was Canon Professor during my last year in the Theology Faculty at Durham University. Even then his twinkling eyes and mobile eyebrows were remarkable. As our Bishop in the 1950s two memories stand out.

During that time there was much public debate about the alleged secret influence of the Freemasons on church appointments and it was even whispered that Michael was a member of them. I remember hearing him make a public disclaimer of membership or subjection to their influence. I think it was at the opening meeting of the Lightfoot Society for Theological Study.

After Bishop Michael moved to York, his successor, Bishop Harland, arranged a residential conference at Butlins, Filey. Bishop Harland was notorious for his ability to forget the name of the cleric he had just instituted! Archbishop Michael stood on the main thoroughfare of the camp and greeted all of us by name arriving from Durham Diocese! Bishop Michael had no small talk and entertaining him in the Vicarage before a confirmation was an agonizing fidget! The late Canon Alan Lazonby, once his chaplain, told me that if AMR received unpleasant letters with which he was reluctant to deal he would slide them down the upholstery of his large easy chair. Alan would have to rescue them and deal with them. A Lovably Human Bishop!

My late stepmother told me that Michael and my father were mutual 'confessors' to each other and would 'cox and box' at the stool of penance. I heard the old sexton at Frosterley, where my father died in office, say of AMR after he had heard him preach, "Yon's a clever man. Did you notice that he never used a word of more than three syllables!" I think that sums up AMR's gift for explaining the most profound truths in simple but moving language.

Joyce says: In 1942 I was a student at St Mary's College and living in what is now the Chorister School. Leaving the Cathedral after the early Eucharist one weekday I was amazed to see AMR and his secretary Joan hand-in-hand ahead of me through the Cloisters. As I looked through the Times as I waited for breakfast, there was the announcement of their engagement. *(The Revd Hilary and Mrs Joyce Jackson)*

Many years ago I was on the French Town Twinning Committee for Bishop Auckland. Each year when the French children visited, Bishop Ramsey invited them to see the castle at Bishop Auckland. The children were from a communist area and asked many questions. The Bishop was unfailingly good humoured and welcoming.

On one occasion my husband and I were at a wine and cheese evening at the castle. My husband went to help a lady struggling to open a window. It was Mrs Ramsey, again a really nice person.

Many years ago my son read the lesson at Whitworth Church, County Durham when Bishop Ramsey was preaching. Of course he found time to say, "well done", and chat to a young boy.

Bishop Ramsey and his wife were people in tune with the people they were living among and were much loved and admired. *(Mrs A Fisher)*

In August of this year I was able, at last, at the age of 84, to visit Durham and to see the magnificent Cathedral. While I was there I spoke to one of your number about my recollections of Michael Ramsey, whom I remember from my childhood in Boston in Lincolnshire. Mr Ramsey, was early in his career, one of the curates at Boston Parish Church, I think at one time he may have been the lecturer.

At any rate he taught me when I was a member of the junior congregation (teenagers) at St James' Church. St James' was a small Victorian church, now pulled down, which was attached to St Botolph's and I imagine that Mr Ramsey at one time was priest-in-charge. St Botolph's in those days often had several curates, not so nowadays of course. Sunday School at St James' took place in the church hall, but older children became members of the junior congregation and moved into the Church itself on Sunday afternoons, where the boys sat on the left hand pews, and the girls on the right.

Mr Ramsey was not the ideal person to be in charge of a group of teenagers, most of whom were in church only to give their parents an afternoon rest after Sunday lunch. There was quite a lot of talking among the young people and knowing winks and nods from the boys across the middle aisles, to try and attract the girls. Mr Ramsey put up with this lack of attention for a while, but where other curates might have come down heavily on the offenders, Ramsey employed another solution—he knelt down and prayed!

Whether he was praying to prevent him showing anger, or to ask God for help, I do not know, but it worked like magic. The offenders were so embarrassed that they quietened down immediately, and I don't remember any repetition while he was in charge. It must be about 70 years ago, but I have never forgotten it!

Mr Ramsey took his duties very seriously; he was the only curate that I can remember actually paying visits to the people in the parish. Unfortunately he had no small talk at all, so I did not particularly enjoy coming home from school to find Mr Ramsey taking tea with my mother, she being as nervous and lost for words as her visitor. On one occasion, I pulled out my Latin homework, which prompted an enthusiastic response from Mr Ramsey. It was probably the only thing in our house that he could relate to!

It was a pity that my father was at work when Mr Ramsey came visiting, as he really appreciated his scholarship and was very impressed when Mr Ramsey came to Boston and knew he would go far. My father left school at 14 and spent his working life as a clerk on the railway, but he loved the church and spent his years of retirement looking after the old books in St Botolph's Parish Church Library. *(Margaret Lee)*

There was a butler to the Bishops of Durham, Ernie Alexander, my mother's uncle. He lived with a daughter. He had a book published after he retired; still living in the apartments. 'My 53 years as Butler to the Bishop of Durham'. *(Reg Lethbridge)*

I met him to speak to for the first time on 23rd August 1975 when he was living in Cuddesdon. I was on leave from Kitwe in Zambia and visiting Cuddesdon. Driving into the village along the lanes I suddenly saw his unmistakable shape and amble. He was wearing a purple shirt and a 'straw basher' and he carried a forked walking stick. I stopped the car and greeted him and explained that I was 'home' from Kitwe in Zambia. "Ah, yes", he said, "St Michael's. I remember it well". He was there in 1960. I was astonished that he could recollect a place quite out of the blue. In 1977 he preached at Stockton Parish Church, Cleveland. We spoke again and he clearly remembered me from that chance encounter.

The last time I met him was in Durham at St John's College. It was some sort of social do. I had just called on Ben de la Mare at St Oswald's Vicarage. I don't know why I said it but I implied more or less that Ben would keep his eye on him. "I don't need anyone to keep an eye on me", he replied. That sort of ended a rather hopeless conversation.

There is the 'silver story' It was he and Joan's first evening at Auckland Castle. Used to his predecessor's style, the butler enquired of the Ramsey silver. There was a long silence and then fidgety conversation between he and Joan. After a further lengthy pause he said, "Ah, the silver....It's in the bank". *(The Rt Revd Stephen Pedley)*

Catching one's eye as one enters the Anglican Centre in Rome today is a large framed photograph of two elderly men bent towards each other, hands touching, wrought with obvious emotion.

The moment captured was in March 1966. The place was Rome, during Archbishop Michael Ramsey's visit only months after the conclusion of the Second Vatican Council. The occasion was an ecumenical service at St Paul's Outside the Walls *[Italian: Basilica Papale di San Paolo fuori le Mura— Editor]*, where Pope Paul VI and Archbishop Michael Ramsey had prayed together. There, following the service, Pope Paul VI gave the episcopal ring from his time as Archbishop of Milan to Michael Ramsey.

Archbishop Ramsey's Chaplain, John Andrew, had been asked the previous evening whether the Archbishop should be forewarned.

Conferring, it was agreed the gift should come as a surprise. As John Andrew describes it, the Pope asked the bemused Archbishop to remove his ring; John Andrew had to prompt him to do so, then the Pope took his own ring off and placed it in Ramsey's hand. The Archbishop looked at it, looked again, and burst into tears. The Pope placed his arms around him to provide some privacy, and rummaged in his pocket to hand him his handkerchief.

Later the ring box was handed to John Andrew. He thought at the time: "The Archbishop won't need it, he will never take the ring off." He gave the box instead to the Anglican Centre as a memento. And much later still, after Ramsey's death, the ring itself was given to the Archbishops of Canterbury, who wear it still when they make an official visit to the Vatican.

Archbishop Michael Ramsey and Pope Paul VI (1966)
(Photo courtesy of The Anglican Centre in Rome)

Virginia Johnstone, then secretary to Canon John Findlow, the first Director of the Anglican Centre, recalls other snippets of the visit. The Archbishop took a lift to the then largely bare rooms of the new Anglican Centre in the Palazzo Doria Pamphilj to dedicate the chapel. She recalls her own difficulty having any kind of conversation with him, but later his great success with the students of the Venerable English College, who cheered him as he threw his Canterbury cap into the air. Ordinary Italians also warmed to him and his escorted car was cheered as he drove through the streets of Rome.

The placement of the iconic photograph in pride of place in the Anglican Centre is deliberate: the friendship and affection it expresses between these two visionary leaders, as much as their prayer together and their inauguration of formal dialogues between the two communions, foreshadowed the study, education, prayer and fostering of friendship and affection which has undergirded the Anglican Centre from its dedication by the Archbishop that March in 1966 to the present day.

The current Director of the Anglican Centre, David Richardson, as a teenager, was Archbishop Michael's Server in St John's Cathedral, Brisbane, and recalled his difficulty years later keeping the Archbishop in one piece when he gave a teaching week based at Great St Mary's in the late 1970s: "Mind your head, Your Grace, this doorway is very low." "Yes, yes, yes." Crash! *(Margie Richardson, The Anglican Centre in Rome)*

The Bailey hung with that particular autumnal fog that was so exclusive to Durham; part mist from the river valley and part soggy damp low cloud shrouding the Cathedral heights, infused with the taste of coal tar from the open fires of the surrounding pit villages. Out of the gloom coalesced a black clad figure, dew drops of moisture clinging to the cobwebs of his hair; a gruff morning greeting and he passed, almost silently, his steps muffled on the leafy cobbles.

My first term at Durham (1980) and my first meeting with the former Archbishop of Canterbury, Michael Ramsey. So began our almost daily encounters. Depending on the exact time of day, he was returning from early morning prayer at the Cathedral or from celebrating mass at St Chad's and I was gambolling along to a tutorial or seminar in my department at Saddler Street. I had, of course, recognised him immediately. A figure from history, exactly like his image on the grainy black and white film of the Queen's Coronation. Seemingly ancient. We were after all, children of the Silver Jubilee, a whole generation beyond that. After all, the 'past was another country', according to the popular literature. Gradually and almost imperceptibly, Lord Ramsey became part of my life. He noticed that I often attended Evensong and especially that when the other students went down at the end of term, I stayed up for as long as was possible. He tackled me about this one day, as it had obviously concerned him, stopping me on Prebends' Bridge to ask, in a pastoral way, if I was alright. He suspected that perhaps there was some sort of trouble at home or maybe an angst filled love interest. Mundanely I explained that I came from a small Cornish village, which had no facilities, took all day to reach and seemed totally uninspiring and crucially had no access to books. The University Library was my lifeline.

Sympathetically he questioned me about the difficulty of working without books to reference and tentatively asked me if I knew anything about the nineteenth-century North Cornish cleric, known as Parson Hawker, as he was an admirer of the eccentric clergyman. As luck would have it, the Revd S. Hawker, Parson Hawker's father, had been vicar of my parish church and 'Parson' had grown up knowing the same houses and lanes as I had. An invitation to tea was swiftly issued, in order to cement a new-found common interest. Something of an ordeal at first, these then regular afternoons gradually relaxed into hugely enjoyable occasions, when all manner of things were discussed, albeit with erudition one side and gauche enthusiasm on the other. Studying archaeology meant that the topic of the Early Church had a great attraction as did the Rule of St Benedict and the lives of Cuthbert, Aidan and Bede. But the maverick Vicar of Morwenstowe, a very human character, was never far away. What could a great theologian find in a humble Cornish clergyman to intrigue and entertain him endlessly? Certainly Hawker **was** a character, the stuff of myth and legend, forever associated with instigating Harvest Festivals and stories of 'wrecking' — or more accurately of episodes of saving the souls of seafarers. He wrote lush poems in the Romantic style, composed hymns and his ballad, 'The Song of the Western Men', otherwise known as 'Trelawney', is the unofficial Cornish national anthem, representing as it does rebellion against authority.

Perhaps M'Lord recognised the outstanding humanity and humility of the man, who welcomed animals into his church as if it were the ark, buried seafarers of all nationalities at his own expense and empathised with his poverty stricken parishioners saying, "If I eat and drink, and see my poor hunger and thirst, I am not a minister of Christ, but a lion that lurketh in his den to ravish the poor." Or possibly he saw Hawker as the embodiment of mission, what the modern church calls 'faith in action'. A man who lived his words in deeds and who thought little of money or its attendant trappings; although he had one affection of note. Over his shoulders he wore a stole, which he had made for him, to replicate that found in the coffin of St Cuthbert at Durham. Parson Hawker had a special reverence for the memory of this saint, who lived a life of prayer and meditation on an equally wild coast, occupying a position he felt, not unlike his own.

Lord Ramsey had the profound gift of great educators, that of imparting knowledge without appearing to teach and preaching without turning doctrine into dictats. His generosity of spirit manifested itself in diverse ways, both practical and cerebral and in conversation he had the ability of the consummate sermon writer, that of making the particular universal and both fresh and exciting. He let people discover things for themselves and celebrated this with them. An intensely private man, it was several months before I realised that his 'housekeeper' who fed me so very well, was in fact his beloved wife, as no endearments were ever exchanged in front of me; he was by turns funny and endearing, compassionate and moved to tears by injustice and cruelty. His charm and rhetoric ensured that any debate was a masterpiece of intellect and profound thought. His meditation at the Union Society on the topic of 'Is God a Myth?' was a tour de force and simply legendary!

But above all, my personal memory is of a humble man, a man who still wore gaiters when they were more than old fashioned, but whose thinking was never antiquated. He had had radical positive beliefs concerning homosexuals and women in the church and foresaw the inevitability of women in the episcopate, 'as night follows day'.

Doubtless many others can highlight Michael Ramsey's place in the history of the church and his penetrating theological mind; I can only reflect on his many kindnesses to me, as both an undergraduate and postgraduate. Being taken under his wing, albeit in a small way, had a profound influence on my thinking and my work as an archaeologist and I hope that his place in Durham's history will not be forgotten. *(Nicola Trzaska-Nartowski)*

The Ramsey cope *[This is not the Coronation Cope—Editor]* was probably made in 1953 in the style of Victorian arts and crafts, with matching mitre and a Cuthbert Cross hood. The full set included matching veil and burse in the same arts and crafts style.

Examples of mitres with coronets can be found in the crossing of the Cathedral and Bishop Ramsey had previously remarked about the Bishops of Durham being Prince Bishops and that in the past he would have been wearing a crown or coronet. A second mitre with a coronet was made which Bishop Michael Ramsey wore, and when he was transferred to York a second hood was made with the Cross Keys on it, so he could wear this at York.

After the death of Michael Ramsey the cope, mitres and hoods were given to Durham Cathedral. When Bishop David Jenkins was at Durham, he rather admired the cope and wore it on several occasions; he even took it back to Auckland Castle with him and the Chapter had to ask for it back! *(Maureen Martin)*

My first awareness of Michael Ramsey is when I was eight and his appointment as the next Archbishop of Canterbury was announced early in 1961. This caused my parents much pleasure and satisfaction as they both knew him well, my father as a University colleague when Ramsey was Van Mildert Professor and Canon Residentiary at Durham University and Cathedral respectively from 1940-50, and my mother as a user of Durham University Library where she was Acting/Deputy Librarian for much of Ramsey's time.

Soon after his appointment to Canterbury, one of my aunts caught mumps and was meanly teased that she looked like the Archbishop-designate.

Later the same year another aunt married a retired bishop who had been present at the Coronation in 1953 and had a copy of the Coronation painting, so on our next visit the unmistakable figure of the then Bishop of Durham was pointed out to us so that, when in June 1963 the BBC screened the recording of the Coronation on the 10th anniversary, we were able to pick him out easily in his exalted position on the Queen's left hand.

In April that year we watched him 'in action' on television conducting Princess Alexandra's wedding in Westminster Abbey, but the bride and Royal guests were much more interesting.

On 13th June 1967 Archbishop Ramsey came to Durham to open Van Mildert College and the front page of the student union newspaper, 'Palatinate', of 15th June carried a superb photo, entitled 'His Ghostly Grace', of a semi-transparent Archbishop superimposed on the distinctive College buildings.

The next Royal wedding conducted by Ramsey was that of Princess Anne and Captain Mark Phillips, which took place on 14th November 1973, Ramsey's 69th birthday, and I thought it rather tough that he had to spend his birthday on such an activity.

By curious coincidence, since I was unaware that he had briefly been incumbent there some 35 years earlier, when I was a student in Cambridge I happened to go to Evening Prayer at St Benet's on 15th May 1974 at the end of a particularly stressful day, only to learn that Ramsey was to retire on his 70th birthday that November.

A cousin of my mother, Hugh Whitworth, became the Archbishop's Lay Advisor in 1969 and I was fascinated to learn from him that Ramsey was wont in meetings to appear to doze off only to 'wake up' when everyone else had bogged themselves down in discussion and draw everything to a neat and extremely well-considered conclusion. Hugh was greatly impressed by this skill.

Late in 1978 I returned to live in Durham and soon afterwards was introduced by my father to Michael Ramsey, who had himself returned to live in Durham the previous year. Despite this I do not remember greeting him when I encountered his distinctive figure moving in a stately fashion round the city, since I concluded that he would be unlikely to remember who I was.

Over the following years Michael Ramsey and his wife again, as they had in the 1940s, took part in Durham Cathedral and University life. They attended Sung Eucharist at 11.30 on Sundays, despite increasing infirmity, until they left Durham for Bishopthorpe in 1986. He rejoined the men's discussion group, 'The Quick and the Dead', which had been founded in the 1930s by a group of clergy and dons, led by his predecessor as Canon Professor, Oliver Quick. He was included in processions at special services, though as a member of the University, which had accorded him the status of Emeritus Professor, thus relieving the Cathedral of the difficult problem of what to do with a retired Archbishop! He was probably still as unskilled at processing as he seems (according to his biographers) to have been all his life, which perhaps accounts for the story I was told long ago that when he was Canon Professor he erred when processing and Dean Alington threatened to fire him if he did so again, to which Ramsey replied that surely that was what can(n)ons were for!

They had a mature lady help (I assume Audrey Heaton), who dressed in cotton frocks and children's sandals, and who drove them around in—of all the incongruous vehicles—a bright blue Mini Clubman! However, I am actually not surprised that even Michael Ramsey should have fitted into it as I knew someone of 6'4" who found a Mini more spacious and comfortable than several larger cars. *(Clare Wright)*

I was variously Acting and Deputy University Librarian from 1942-50. The University was then, especially in wartime, a small community and the Library staff knew all the dons and they all knew each other, so I knew Michael Ramsey, Van Mildert Professor of Divinity in the University of Durham and Canon Residentiary of Durham Cathedral from 1940-50, and his wife, Joan, well.

The University Library was then housed entirely in what is now the Palace Green section, and the issue desk was located immediately inside the front door at the bottom of the steps. Straight ahead up the steps, where the present-day issue desk is located, was the Reading Room, which had four large reading tables each with a fixed reading lamp with a metal shade in the middle.

My abiding recollection of the then Canon Professor Ramsey is of his arriving in the University Library and habitually placing his hat on top of one of these lamps. He would then go and fetch the books he wanted, sit down at the table and invariably try to pull the lamp towards him! *(Ella Wright)*

I was an undergraduate at St John's from 1980—83 and well remember the familiar figures of the Ramseys walking up and down the Bailey. As someone who was exploring vocation I once asked to go and see Michael prior to going on a personal retreat which I had never done before. He gladly agreed and prior to my arrival had clearly given this some thought as he had prepared a pile of books by his side and after asking me what I had been reading and a little about myself he selected one which he thought most appropriate. It was William Temple's 'Readings in St John's Gospel' (I forget the exact title) directing me to a particular chapter. He sent me away with some gentle guidance about how to use my time and asked me to come back and tell him how I got on. Which I did. Just another example, of I am sure many, of his personal touch and pastoral concern especially for young ordinands. We used to breakfast occasionally with him at St Chad's but, of course, being faced with small talk over bacon and eggs was not his forte, but he got by with simply the vigorous fluttering of his eyebrows, and repetition, repetition, repetition! *(The Revd Ian Hunter Smart)*

The scene is New College, Oxford, in an undergraduate's room in about 1967. A group of students were asking him questions before he preached at Evensong. One answer, to a question which I don't remember, ended, "And... and ... and (x11)... and... so on." *(Andrew Killick)*

Michael Ramsey was very proud of being the successor of the Prince Bishops. On one occasion after he became bishop he was speaking at the lunch held in those days on St Chad's Day in the college of that dedication to an audience which was composed almost entirely of ordained priests or those in training for ordination. In the course of this address he exhorted them to stay in their parishes for a reasonable length of time. Three or four years of learning before they could then 'give' something to their parishes. A year later he was again at the lunch having been appointed Archbishop of York after only three years as Bishop of Durham. He began his speech with a quote from the Psalms 'Put not your trust in princes'. *(David Crookes)*

My father was a Methodist minister in Darlington at the time of the Queen's coronation. Archbishop Ramsey came from a rehearsal at Westminster Abbey to our house on May 26th 1953 to take part in the Bi-Centenary celebrations of the visit of John Wesley. I was a teenage schoolgirl, yet Archbishop Ramsey took an interest in what I was doing—and especially in my homework for that day! He told me about the rehearsal, and treated me as an equal. I have always held him in high regard, and never forgot his visit to our house. *(Hazel Weatherill)*

I remember long ago (the late 1970s to be precise) when I was curate of Boston Stump—the long retired Bishop Ramsey returned to preach at the parish where he had been Lecturer even longer ago (the late 1930s). At the reception in the vicarage after the service we were all enjoying a glass of wine when cameras appeared. Bishop Ramsey turned to me and said "Never be photographed with a glass in your hand"—it is sage advice that I have adhered to throughout 33 years of ministry. *(Father David Reynish)*

Bishop Michael confirmed me shortly before his translation to York—I remember kneeling before him and also his wonderful smile (as well as the discussions prior to the event about the wearing—or not—of our blue 'choir veils'!)

Over the years I continued to admire and respect him for his liberal theological views, support of Anglo-Catholicism and his ecumenism. I certainly came to believe in his vision of hell as being not a physical place but made by people themselves denying God a place in their lives. I can see him still in his appearance on television in 1960 with the Roman Catholic Archbishop of Liverpool, JC Heenan, discussing the meeting between the Archbishop of Canterbury and Pope John XXIII and I remember the joy we felt when we heard he was to become the 100th Archbishop of Canterbury.

A truly great and lovely man. *(Marion Whyte)*

I remember my first meeting with him. I was an undergraduate at St Chad's 1976—79 and, having arrived back from the Library too late for informal Dinner, grabbed my gown and dashed down to get to the Formal Dinner. Unluckily I was spotted by Fr John Fenton, the principal in those days, who ushered me up to fill the empty places at top table. A few minutes later an elderly gentleman sat down beside me. Other than a brief hello nothing was said until after the soup course. I was feeling rather bored by then and the elderly gentleman seemed lost in thought. After a bit I asked if he was at the College. "No" he replied and we lapsed into silence. "So what do you do?" I asked. "Oh I am retired" he replied. "What did you do before you retired?" I persisted? "Oh I was Archbishop of Canterbury" he replied quietly. I was lost for words but never forgot that formal Dinner at St Chad's! *(James MKensie-Hall)*

I was walking up South Street having bought a raffia wastepaper bin. Walking towards me was Michael Ramsey. "What have you got there Dyson?" I told him. "May I examine it?" he said. I gave it to him. Having examined it he put it on his head. "A good hat too don't you think!" He was heart-warmingly playful and his levity was profoundly touching. *(Henry Dyson)*

He was working late in the Lambeth Palace Library, and as the Revd Canon John Andrew passed, he asked, "Could you tell me what time it is, please?", to which John replied, "Bedtime, Father", to which Ramsey responded, "I was asking for information, and not advice." *(The Rt Revd Kenneth Stevenson)*

You are asking for recollections of Michael Ramsey. Mine is of a non-meeting with him; I was travelling back from London on the train and the carriage was nearly empty apart from Michael Ramsey who was sitting on the opposite side of the carriage some two or three seats down from my seat. I made up my mind on at least three occasions to go and introduce myself to him but each time chickened out as I believed that after the initial introduction I would find myself with little conversation with the great man and each time he looked so benevolent but, no, I could not take that first step.

The train arrived in Durham and we both departed on our separate ways. He not knowing who on earth I was and me kicking myself for missing the opportunity of a few words with such a person.

Over the years I have recounted this story to various people who knew him and all said he would have been delighted to have me introduce myself and spend some time in conversation, he was that sort of man. My great loss I am afraid! *(Paul Jefferson)*

I was baptized by Bishop Michael on the feast of St. John the Baptist, 1953, at St Andrew's Church, Tudhoe Grange, Spennymoor. My father was the vicar. It was three weeks after the Queen's coronation and I am informed that the Bishop (who attended on the Queen's right) talked about the ceremony to the godparents. However, my first real memory of Bishop Michael was when my father received a copy of his enthronement sermon at Canterbury. I remember the surprise and delight my father showed. The year must have been 1961.

My next memory is that, after having written to say that I was going to be confirmed, I received a reply. This was on official paper and contained his episcopal signature. I still have this along with its original Sir Winston Churchill stamp. My confirmation was in Durham Cathedral by Bishop Harland in November 1965. Then I remember seeing on the television Bishop Michael in discussion with Pope Paul VI in Rome in the mid sixties; as a teenager, I was aware that something significant was happening but it is only in later years that I have grasped its full meaning.

Lastly, for the latter part of Holy Week and the first part of Easter Week 1994, I went on holiday to Canterbury. Whilst there, I found the plaque to Bishop Michael in Canterbury Cathedral and I photographed it.

The long term effect on me has been that I consider Bishop Michael to have been a Bishop of deep prayer and great learning. I have two of his books: 'Gateway to God, daily readings with Michael Ramsey' and 'Be still and know.' This latter book is about prayer and I recommend it. Both are baptism anniversary presents. I do not think I shall go far wrong in life if I persevere in the same way with my reading. *(Michael Woolstenholmes)*

His lectures were brilliant. I only missed two, because of a heavy cold — and even these I caught up on several decades later! He had the manner of an elderly man — I could hardly believe he was only 20 years and a day older than I. His walk, however was like his age of 43.

Oddly enough, my chief memory of Michael Ramsey was outside the lecture room at St Deiniol's Library, Hawarden, then in Flintshire. It is the National Memorial of Gladstone and in my day, c. 1950, it was residential only for men. I studied there as an undergraduate for some time. To my consternation, I found he was there as an ordinary guest. People were treating him as a fellow guest — but we were somewhat in awe of him at Durham. In fact, I was slightly taken aback when a school friend referred to him as simply "Michael Ramsey". Eventually I approached him and re-introduced myself. I reminded him that I had been thrown out; quite rightly, of Honours Theology as not up to standard then. (Evidently I was a late developer, as I got my master's later on, and eventually a PhD. at Leeds, and for 26 years was Secretary of Durham University Society.)

Those who were leaving the Library were allowed to have an early breakfast. I put in for this, so I could help Professor Ramsey with his luggage for the walk to the railway station—little guessing what his splendid future would be. An anti-climax came when the warden quietly scolded me that early breakfast was for those actually leaving and not for those assisting the departure.

My last meeting with him, then Archbishop, was in a lift at the Centenary Dinner in 1966 for The Durham University Society. He and the Earl of Scarborough, then our Chancellor, were guest speakers. Archbishop Ramsey greeted me with, "You were the Archah, I remembah". *(Dr David Hill)*

When Michael Ramsey was appointed Canon Professor, the first thing that struck the other dons who lived in the Castle was his oddness. The Warden (Vice-Chancellor) Duff assured them that he was now not nearly so odd as he was when he had known him at the choir school of King's College, Cambridge. The Principal of St John's declared roundly that he was a lunatic —"I saw him yesterday afternoon walking down the Bailey with one foot on the pavement and one foot in the gutter all the way". Certainly he waved his arms about more than most men when in action. And most of the seniors had not welcomed the appointment. He was absurdly young. Some of them disliked his book. *['The Gospel and the Catholic Church'—his first book, published in 1936—Editor.]*

They thought that he looked antique, when at rest. He was not yet quite bald, but nearly. He had a grey fringe round back and sides, although a few wisps that had once been fair or ginger were combed over the top. Occasionally he was referred to by those who saw him at services as 'the old canon' though he was much the youngest of the canons. They were privately amused at his clumsiness. In the college at Durham they saw him, as they thought, learning to ride a bicycle; but the truth was that whenever he rode a bicycle he looked as though he was learning to ride.

He visited St Columba's Church in Sunderland where he dedicated the refurbished Lady Chapel. On the top of the wrought iron screen encasing the Lady Chapel were at various intervals the initials 'MR', 'Mary Regina.' It is reported that he remarked "I see you have my initials up there." *(The Revd Canon Arthur Middleton)*

Whitelands College was relocated to Durham during the war. I don't have any particular memories of Michael Ramsey but have spoken to another old Whitelander who can recall him taking some services in Bede College Chapel. All she recalls about the man was seeing him walking down the Bailey with one foot on the kerb and the other in the gutter! She says when his engagement was announced it set the College buzzing. *(Hilda Dixon)*

I came to know Ramsey well in the Michaelmas Term of 1983, when he gave one of the lectures in a series which I had organized for the 150th anniversary of the Oxford Movement. He delivered his lecture on the Oxford Movement in Durham without notes in one of the Elvet Lecture Rooms and subsequently wrote it out and published it. Ramsey was a strange mixture of the forbidding and the kindly; he had no small talk, but you quickly learned to broach with him a serious subject, and he gave you his full attention. He was wholly accessible to Americans on Palace Green, thunderstruck to encounter 'the great Bishop Ramsey'. While he was without any of the modern arts of public relations or 'spin', he was immediately recognisable at once to all Durham old-timers. I was once in the barber shop on the first floor near the Elvet steps: the barber saw him below and all the customers crowded to the window to watch him pass. No subsequent bishop has had a similar local celebrity. He once told me that two sorts of people came to Durham, the upwardly mobile for whom it was a staging post for promotion elsewhere, and the 'burghers', who remained and became citizens. He thought of himself as a burgher, and he was probably in Durham as Professor, Bishop and retiree longer than anywhere else in his long career.

He was, I think, neglected by my Department on his retirement here, in not being asked to do much work for it, and he felt this keenly. He compensated by interesting himself in the ordinands at St Chad's. It was in the St Chad's Senior Common Room that he recited his verses to me on

'The Myth of God Incarnate', a parody of William Blake's 'To Mercy, Pity, Peace, and Love'.

The accompanying note to me sending them to me is dated 5th February 1984. I have kept their original punctuation.

> To Goulder, Cupitt, Nineham[,] Wiles[,]
> all call in their distress,
> in hope that they will lead us 'through
> the Nicene wilderness.
>
> For Goulder says it all began
> with naughty Simon Magus,
> and theories from Samaria
> need not for ever plague us.
>
> And Cupitt thinks it very wrong
> to speak of Incarnation,
> because we should keep separate
> Creator and Creation.
>
> And Wiles thinks all theology
> needs a complete remaking,
> but so far he's not let us know
> what shape this will be taking.
>
> For Nineham says that history
> can't tell what really happened,
> which means that all the theories
> end up a little flattened.

This playfulness could only have been expressed by one long familiar with English Departments of Theology. The 'naughty' ascribed to Simon Magus was a characteristic Ramsey word. I sent a copy of the verses to Owen Chadwick, who has placed them in the Ramsey archive, but Chadwick does not deal with Ramsey's attitude to Anglican Modernism in his biography. I believe that Ramsey saw Stephen Sykes *[The Rt Revd Stephen Sykes, former Bishop of Ely and later Principal of St John's College, Durham—Editor]* as his ultimate successor at York or Canterbury.

I once met Ramsey while I was examining an Oxford DPhil on ARCIC [*The Anglican - Roman Catholic International Commission—Editor*], and asked about the ring given him by Pope Paul VI, originally the gift of the people of Milan. He gave it to me to kiss. I had a long interview with him on the subject, and asked him about his attitude to Evangelical Anglicans. He said that they "had only become important at the end of his ministry", a remarkable statement coming from one reared a Nonconformist. He said of the controversial Bishop Jenkins, "He is not a heretic, but he is a fool, a fool, a fool", and his Anglo-Catholicism had a pronounced liberal strain, especially on any question affecting the freedom of the Church from the State (and vice-versa), a distant consequence, I think, of the Prayer Book controversies of the late 1920s. There is an interesting Michael Ramsey Lecture of 1991 by the great Methodist New Testament scholar Kingsley Barrett, one of Ramsey's Durham colleagues in the 1940s, in which Barrett gently criticises Ramsey for his defence of episcopacy as of the *esse* of the Church.

Ramsey was very short-sighted. Once we stayed in the convent at Bec-Hellouin in Normandy where we were told that, while processing round the church, he had tumbled into the sunken tomb of St Hellouin. Soeur Joseph took pleasure in showing us the room where he and Joan had stayed: she said, "I show you very holy room". Before he left Durham, Ramsey and his wife were nearly blind and, on one occasion, I followed them with some concern down the Bailey as they swerved from one side of the road to the other.

He had an intangible air of holiness, as of someone who said his prayers. This, even more than his intellectual brilliance, was the secret of his influence. He remembered everyone he had ordained which I think was connected with his gift for prayer. *(Dr Sheridan Gilley)*

I first saw Michael Ramsey at the Cathedral of St John the Divine, New York, in the fall of 1962 at the dedication of a new window there. I was on my way to New Haven to begin seminary. After I was ordained and working in the Seattle area I met him when he was here for the General Convention of the Episcopal Church. In the early 1970s I heard him at the

Trinity Institutes *[an annual lecture series organised by Trinity Church—Editor]*, in New York City, and, on one memorable day, the Feast of the Presentation, I heard him preach to a packed church at St Mary the Virgin in NYC. It was at one of the Trinity Institutes, held in Riverside Church, NYC that he invited us all to 'his home'. I am sure I was not alone in thinking that meant tea at Lambeth or in Canterbury. He then went on to say, "and my home is the Gospel of St John." Ever since, when reading or hearing John I have remembered that I am in Michael Ramsey's 'home'. *(Father Ralph Carskadden)*

When I first met Lord Ramsey in the Senior Common Room, after being appointed Chaplain and fellow at Castle, he offered to be my Curate—if that would be acceptable! A little later, enquiring about how we were settling into the North-East, he remarked that we would either love it or hate it, and if after six months we were still talking about 'them' we probably wouldn't stay—but if it was 'us' we might stay forever. The latter has proved (very nearly) the case. On the night that he fell from the dais after High Table ("Good heavens", he said staring at a nearby portrait, "That's Plummer"—and stepped off into space) I escorted him home when his main concern was that his wife, Joan, shouldn't hear about it. Domestic politics. Power behind the enthroned!

As a variant on the well known mis-identification of the omniscient eyebrows, the small daughter of a friend—at the time, Chaplain of Chad's—seeing Ramsey shuffling past her front door asked, in awe, "Mummy is *that* the Dean and Chapter". Told about it afterwards he remarked that he had often been mistaken for God almighty, but never anything as powerful as that!

From his own spirituality: I invited him to preach at a Leavers' Service and he painted a marvellous word-picture of first coming up onto Palace Green, the view of the Castle and Cathedral etc which students would never forget...and finished, "But remember, these things will one day be dust— but I am going to heaven". A pre-NTW *[Nicholas Thomas Wright, former Bishop of Durham—Editor]* formulation perhaps—but one that evidently struck home with his congregation, and apparently, with me. *(The Revd Canon Philip Thomas)*

I was one of the Seminarians at Nashotah House Seminary in Wisconsin when His Grace offered a special course on the theme of the Transfiguration. In his retirement he and Lady Ramsey were part of the seminary community for all three years of my time there. Lady Ramsey and I had a joint interest in Dandie Dinmont Terriers and she was delighted to find someone who not only appreciated this old English breed of dog but actually owned one!

His Grace flew to Kansas to preach at my ordination to the diaconate in April of 1978. Lady Ramsey made her way through the aisle on the return flight sharing a large box of cookies that someone had given her as a gift. I wondered how many of the passengers had any idea who that woman was offering them a cookie!

There are so many favourite Ramsey tales to share but one that is so typical of Lord Ramsey's sense of humour is from a television interview that was taking place on a bench outside what was called 'Lambeth West' or the Ramsey flat at Nashotah House. The reporter asked the magenta-wearing hierarch if he also wore a 'large hat'. He asked her to wait just one moment. Having recently been gifted with a large Texas-style cowboy hat His Grace emerged from the flat wearing the new gift and asking: "Is this the one that you mean?" *(The Very Revd Dr Chad Hatfield)*

When the Ramseys lived in South Bailey, the top floor of their house was a separate flat occupied by Cyril Watson, a master at the Chorister School. He had a washing machine that was notorious for disgorging water which dripped into the Ramsey's house. When this happened, Michael would phone upstairs and, in a quivering voice, ask, "Is there a problem upstairs. There's rather a lot of water in our rooms." We used to get Choristers to take him a birthday cake on his birthday. *(A member of the Cathedral community)*

16 South Bailey, the Ramsey's second retirement home in Durham

In October 1952 I was in the first four months of my National Service based in Aldershot. I was waiting to be posted, on draft for Korea, but this suddenly changed to Suez. At short notice I was given weekend leave and headed for home in Washington, County Durham, still in uniform. I managed to catch, by the skin of my teeth, the last train north from King's Cross and paid the additional cost for the luxury of the Tyne Tees Pullman (7&6d—37.5p). However that meant I had insufficient funds from my remaining 2d (0.75p) to pay for dinner. Nevertheless I found myself a seat at a two-seat table in the dining car joining an older gentleman. When the time came for the waiter to take my order for dinner I hid my embarrassment at my lack of funds by stating I was not hungry. My travel companion swiftly guessed my predicament and challenged my reason for not eating. I confirmed his assertion that I lacked funds. Without any further comment to me he indicated to the waiter that he would pay for my meal. I do not recall what I ate save it was soup and a main course followed by coffee, and that it was significantly better than Army food (even though I was a trainee chef in the catering corps).

We discussed my Army and life experiences, he told me he had been attending a religious conference and in due course I became aware of my benefactor's identity, Bishop Michael, the newly consecrated Bishop of Durham.

When we reached Durham Bishop Michael departed wishing me the best of luck. I thanked him for his kindness and continued on to Newcastle feeling well fed and most grateful. *(Frank Jefferson) [de-la-Noy includes a recollection by Hampton Gervis that Ramsey was short of money at school and often went without jam, so they paid him for help with Classics and he probably spent the money in the tuck shop. It is possible that memories of the experience of not having money for food influenced Ramsey to help on this occasion. Editor. See de-la-Noy page 49]*

Memories of Michael Ramsey are mainly because I have lived in his former house in South Street for 25—30 years now. Lord Ramsey had bought the house from Paddy Surtees and had lived in the house for two years. Lord Ramsey went to the 8.00 a.m. service every morning, and in winter had several nasty falls. To make things easier, Lady Ramsey asked the Cathedral if they had a house available closer to the Cathedral and signed an agreement to move into a house on the Bailey which was suitable for them.

I had come back from Africa and wanted to live somewhere closer to town. I heard that the house in South Street was up for sale and, with the encouragement of the Cathedral's Land Agent, wrote Lord Ramsey a letter saying I would be interested in buying his house as I would have liked to be near my students. This apparently was the right thing to say! Joan Ramsey showed me around the house, we went upstairs to two beautiful attic bedrooms. One of the bedrooms was made into a chapel; the fireplace had been made into an altar, with two prayer stools and a large collection of icons round the walls. The other bedroom was small and contained all of Lord Ramsey's vestments. Lady Ramsey's sitting room faced the Cathedral. Downstairs was Lord Ramsey's library which was lined with books right up to the rail and a separate pier going out, his desk was set to look into the garden. None of the good rooms in the house faced onto the Cathedral, the best view was from the attic bedrooms. Lord Ramsey's bedroom was at the back so that he couldn't hear the bells. The spare bedroom was on the first floor facing the Cathedral and was very small, I don't think they had very much money to spend on decoration but it was very nicely decorated. I said, "Nice but a bit small" Lady Ramsey replied, "You don't want to make your guests too comfortable". Which I thought was quite amusing.

50 South Street, the Ramseys' first retirement home in Durham

The Ramseys had a housekeeper and a small section of the kitchen had been cut off for her. Her bedsit had a toilet, washbasin and shower and she had access to the garden to watch the two terriers go and make a mess. In Lord Ramsey's garden there was a wooden house which had been given to him by the previous people on his retirement.

I only saw Lord Ramsey in the hall in passing, going outwards. The Estate Agent, who had a reputation for forcing up prices, asked me afterwards, "Do you want the house?" It was a lot of money for me but I liked it and my bank manager encouraged me so I said that I couldn't afford any more than the asking price and not a penny more. The agent said, "Lord Ramsey likes you and would like you to have the house. If you can meet the asking price, it is yours." I think he liked me because I had said I wanted to be near my students—something very important to him.

The view of the garden from the position of Michael Ramsey's desk in South Street.

After I had agreed to buy it, Lady Ramsey said to me, "Would you like to measure up for curtains and carpets? Here is a key we shall be out on Thursday morning. You can look round." I walked into the large study and sat in the armchair by the fireplace, to get the feel of the place, I knew I wanted it, it felt like home.

We had a little house warming and the Ramseys came, I said, "Would you like to see what I have done to Lady Ramsey's sitting room?" Michael stood by my desk looked round and said, "Yes, yes, a place to work."

Subsequently, one day there was a knock at the door. I opened it and there was Joan Ramsey standing there looking rather puzzled with a letter in her hand. She couldn't remember where the letter box was. It was in the tradesman's entrance, immediately next to the front door, but presumably she never picked up letters, leaving that to the housekeeper.

Lord Ramsey was a member of several colleges, and Joan was his secretary. Some people found him difficult to talk to but I found him very easy. At first he didn't seem to know that he had to sign for drinks at SCR dinners. I remember he fell down two steps flat on his face, and everyone froze. Somebody picked him up and he said, "Don't tell the wife".

In my car we had a conversation about Prime Ministers. His favourite was Harold Macmillan, he went through all of the Prime Ministers but didn't mention Harold Wilson.

Michael was very fond of walking, when it was raining he would walk round the inside of the Cathedral.

I commented that the Queen would not have known that he had moved, Joan said, "She should have done, I told her so". *(Dr Dai Morgan)*

About Miss Heaton and her dogs: she used to bring them to Evensong at St Oswald's, and parked them under the pew and they always very well behaved. I started preaching, and one of the dogs barked right in the middle of my sermon; I was startled as I had no idea they were there, the congregation collapsed with laughter. *(Alan Piper)*

I was a student member of the University, 1949—53 at St Hild's College, as well as being born and bred in County Durham, and have fond memories of 'Michael our Bishop' as we always referred to him.

I can always see him, in my mind's eye, processing towards the Quire and his throne, escorted by two little probationer choristers (one at each side) in their purple cassocks and Eton collars. Each carried something for their bishop (his bible, I think, and what else? Something for his head, other than his mitre??)

Whenever I sit in the Quire Stalls, I look across, to his throne, remembering and 'seeing' him there. I can see him seated on his high throne, looking down on us—his bright intelligent eyes twinkling and observing everything, and his bushy eyebrows 'twitching'. Delightful!

I can see him seated in an old armchair in a common room at St.Hild's—as a guest of SCM, on a Sunday night—with students around him and sitting at his feet, hanging on his every word. He was totally relaxed and at ease among students—like a grandfather, no stammer!

I can see him on a Saturday afternoon, in a packed Woolworths in Silver Street, just walking around the store, observing and mingling in with the shoppers, pausing to speak occasionally to one or two of them. Would they know who he was, I wonder?

My parental home was in Crook, and my parish church was St Catherine's. I can see him at a Confirmation service there. By no means was he a proud, aloof 'prince of the Church'. Instead, he again was a loving grandfatherly figure to those young people; and when he gave his address, he stood at the crossing, close to the candidates and their families (not elevated in the pulpit). He spoke to them (a mining community) directly, in clear and simple language—a true Christian pastor as opposed to the brilliant scholar and theologian that I knew he was. Everyone spoke so warmly about him after the service, and for years to come. A true shepherd of his flock.

This last sentence brings me to a memory of my mother! For 60 years she was a devoted (b. 1901) member of the MU [*Mother's Union—Editor*]. Right up to her mid 80s, she recalled a wonderful day when 'Michael our Bishop' led his flock across the sands (before the tarmac road was laid) to Holy Island on a Mother's Union annual pilgrimage. The weather was perfect. The M.U. banners were unfolded—and there was Michael, barefoot, trousers rolled up, leading his flock and virtually paddling!- and happily mingling with the devoted ladies once on dry land in picnic groups after the simple service.

Canon Alan Richardson was my personal tutor for theology, and with two other Hildites I would attend weekly seminars in his home in The College. It was the time of the Queen's Coronation. 'Canon Dicky' told us how the canons wives were longing to hear all about the new Queen when he returned to Durham. He was such an unworldly man, and all he could tell them was, "She's a nice young thing"! Nothing about what she wore etc!! I love to see replays of the crowning, with Michael at her side.

Some people recall his stammer. This disappeared when he was with students and with the ordinary parishioners.

On formal occasions and reception, for example in his York days he was ill at ease and had no small talk (and with this I empathise whole heartedly!) But among his flock, he came into his own. *(Joan M. Putz nee Harrison)*

When I came to St Mary's College as Principal we were without a chaplain in my first year. In those days, the student Chapel committee was very active and invited a range of people to take services. It was usual to have a service of Holy Communion once a term and Michael Ramsey was invited to take a service which attracted more students than usual, although in those days services were well-attended. I remember that as I knelt next to Joan Ramsey in the Chapel, I heard a student rushing down the aisle saying in a loud whisper, "We'd better go to the kitchen and get some more bread." Over breakfast, he and Joan told me how much they had valued their association with St Mary's College and with Miss Fergusson.

No doubt someone at the Cathedral may know that wonderful story of Michael Ramsey in his retirement, emerging from the shadows in the Cathedral to speak in hushed tones to tourists who thought he was dead— or at least that was how the story went and perhaps he told it himself. *(Joan Kenworthy)*

The Michael Ramsey memorial lectures were instituted at the suggestion of Joan Kenworthy, Principal of St Mary's College from 1977—99. She writes, 'They took the form of an annual sermon or lecture in the Chapel of St Mary's College in memory of his association with the college, as Chaplain when the college was in the Cathedral and he was Canon Professor, and as a friend to the college in his retirement in Durham. ... I wrote for advice to Professor Jones, then in retirement in Scotland, having heard his very moving eulogy at the memorial service in the Cathedral. His advice was simple, "Consult Canon Professor Dan Hardy." [*Former Van Mildert Professor at Durham University and a former Canon at Durham Cathedral — Editor*]. To my surprise and delight his response too was simple, he had consulted the Department of Theology and the Dean and Chapter and they wished to join the college in pursing the idea. ... The lectures became very special events with a big dinner in college afterwards. ... In the choice of speakers, the committee was concerned to represent the theology and ideas of Michael Ramsey, to include some people who had known him in his earlier years, and to include representatives of denominations other than Anglican as that would have pleased him. The more humble plan for events in the College Chapel was intended as a tribute to the memory of Michael Ramsey from the college. Perhaps the lecture series came to an end because it was so ambitious, but it was a fitting memorial and tribute from Durham itself.'

Some extracts from lectures which give insights into Michael Ramsey himself include:

While at Durham, Ramsey published two more books on the New Testament, 'The Resurrection of Christ' and 'The Glory of God and the Transfiguration of Christ.' ... The book on Glory and Transfiguration looks to me like Ramsey's farewell to New Testament study—that is, to New Testament study as an end in itself; it would be quite misleading to suggest that he ever ceased to look to the New Testament as the ultimate source of all theological thinking. Indeed, if I may be allowed a personal reference, I shall never forget that when, in retirement, Ramsey returned to his beloved Durham, he returned to the New Testament seminar which in the 1940s I had persuaded him to found and over which I now, in the 1970s, presided, and sat among us with his Greek New Testament before him, never obtruding himself but offering from time to time his mature reflection on the text we were studying. *(Professor Charles Kingsley Barrett, 'Theology in Durham in the Ramsey period', The Michael Ramsey Memorial Lecture, St Mary's College, University of Durham 1991 p6)*

...So it came about that in July 1932, I, along with some 40 others, was coming to terms with the subwarden at Lincoln, himself a Cuddesdon man, who had arrived there after a curacy in Liverpool. This was not at all straightforward, for he was an eccentric, a genuine, not a contrived, eccentric. He walked with a swaying gait; and although he came to have more practice at it than most he never mastered the processional walk in church. His voice had ascending and descending cadences, which could become sing-song, and one had to learn by experience that his repeated, "yes, yes, yes" might in fact mean, "no". As eloquent as the voice were the eyebrows; and only this year I met a woman Lutheran pastor from the United States who dates life from the day when, as a little girl in pigtails, she was allowed to climb up on his knee, remove his spectacles and play with the eyebrows. We were told that he had been president of the Cambridge Union in record time, and that Asquith had referred to him as the future leader of the Liberal Party. This we could hardly credit until one day in the long vacation term, I imagine through boredom, we decided to hold a debate on the motion that 'this House disapproves of His Majesty's government', and the subwarden was persuaded to propose the motion. Then for 20 minutes the visor was raised, and we were treated to a superlative display of political oratory. Then the visor was lowered and we never saw the like again.

Holiness, then, I would judge to have been a second initial and basic ingredient in Michael Ramsey's mental and spiritual make-up. That it continued as a *leit-motif* can also be shown from his scattered writings; but first, in view of a certain glibness which can so easily attach to the subject, let me quote from a sermon he once preached in a Sunderland parish. The occasion was the commissioning of a group of nuns to serve in the parish and, having commented on that, he turned to address the general congregation to the effect that the monastic vocation was but one form of the vocation to holiness to which they were all called as Christians; and he continued with these words, "It is terribly hard to put into words just what this holiness means. It is a matter of you and your relation to our Lord; how you are towards him in the depths of your being."

... One of the themes of 'The Gospel and the Catholic Church' had been that the gospel of the death and resurrection of Christ should result in the death of Christian denominations as to their separate existence and their resurrection to a greater wholeness, which one of his critics dismissed contemptuously with the words, "If you can believe that, you can believe anything." He did continue so to believe, particularly in relation to Methodists, with whom in his Durham periods he had fallen in love. Invited to speak at the Bi-Centenary of Methodism in Darlington in 1953 he opened by celebrating the existing measure of unity by giving thanks for John Wesley, and especially for his passion for holiness and zeal in winning souls, and he concluded by an appeal for a greater unity, when, "the shame of denominationalism has been conquered" by quoting Wesley's own words, "We are called to propagate scriptural religion through the land: that is faith working by love, holy tempers and holy lives." Almost twenty years later, in 1972, it fell to him as president of the General Synod of the Church of England to propose the motion to approve a scheme of union between the Church of England and the Methodist Church, already approved by the latter, and he did so in a speech which I can only judge a masterly combination of oratorical skill and spiritual passion. When the teller went to inform him of the voting figures which meant that the motion had failed he burst into uncontrollable weeping. And when by chance he was billed that same evening as the speaker at the annual banquet given by the Lord Mayor of London for the bishops of the Church of England he rose to his feet and said, "Today is the most disgraceful day I have ever spent during my life as a member of the Church of England", and sat down. There had been for him a grave defect in holiness. *(Professor Christopher F Evans 'Humanity, Holiness—and Humour'. The Michael Ramsey Memorial Lecture, St Mary's College, University of Durham 1995 p 1,6.)*

Durham for a variety of ...reasons ... has a special place in my affections. ... It was then that the figure of Michael Ramsey walking across Palace Green, 'The Patriarch' they called him, evoked the comment of a woman bystander, "He's part of the stones around here. I think he is just growing into his face."

When the bishops gave him a dinner in Oxford at the time of his retirement from Canterbury, he replied to a toast which was proposed by Ronald

Williams, sometime principal of St John's College, then the Bishop of Leicester. Those of us who were in that candlelit hall will never forget the way in which he 'took off' and spoke for 20 minutes without hesitation. It was an enchanting dream he had of his arrival in heaven at a sherry party given by former Archbishops. One by one they all came up to talk to him — and they each said something which was in the character of the man's memory. Cranmer, I recall, said to him, "Ramsey, I don't think much of Series III" — and Becket wondered why he had been turned into poetry by a man called Eliot who seemed to figure more in Anglican sermons than God. Or his old headmaster Fisher, "Still Beta Plus Ramsey!" But there was at the end a little man who came up whom he immediately recognised as Anselm. "When we met we embraced each other because here, I felt, there was a man who was primarily a don, who tried to say his prayers and cared nothing for the pomp and glory of his position." We saw that in this picture of Anselm he spoke a portrait of his own ideal for himself.

Of one thing I am sure, on the basis of many long hours spent in the company of Michael Ramsey in places that he loved, especially Cambridge and Cuddesdon, his happiest days were spent here in Durham: close to Cuthbert and Bede. They were days when he was the don who said his prayers untroubled by any pomp or glory of position. *(The Rt Revd Robert Runcie, 'Cantaur and the mission of St Augustine in 597.' The Michael Ramsey Memorial Lecture, St Mary's College University of Durham 1997 p1, 15)*

Many must have memories of him in retirement (as I have), humble, friendly, humorous, brave about old age, and absorbed in worship as a member of the congregation, with a face like a medieval carving of God the Father; and he has an assured place in English history as the hundredth but most unusual Archbishop of Canterbury. *(David L Edwards. 'The Great Christian Centuries to Come'. 'The Michael Ramsey Memorial Lecture,' St Mary's College, the University of Durham 1998. p1)*

We don't have too many memories of Michael Ramsey, though we recall him ambling round Durham in our early days, with tourists etc going "Ooh ah!" when they saw him. I also recall a lecture he gave on whatever anniversary (150 years?) it was of the Oxford Movement, when despite his advanced years he lectured fluently and without notes (so far as I could see). But my favourite memory is of a visit MR made to Nottingham University campus, which must have been in the 70s. The then Vice-Chancellor was present. He was not very popular—had been brought in to run a tight ship, if I recall aright. But he made an effort to show that he was familiar with MR's theme, which I can't recall, and asked a question about "the immaculate conception". To which MR replied in his characteristic style, with arms awave, and awash with courtesy, "I think you mean the virgin birth". Collapse of stout party and muffled hilarity all round. *(Professor Jimmy Dunn)*

My first memory of Michael Ramsey—and it is still after 60 years very vivid—is of his very great kindness to me when I was in Durham to be interviewed for the theology lectureship to which I was appointed in 1950. I was tremendously impressed by his humility and gentleness. Sadly for me, he left Durham for Cambridge before I moved to Durham.

But my impression of him was powerfully confirmed by the strong sense I had of his continuing influence on the department's spirit and its way of doing things. His influence was somehow an abiding element of our life and work together and an extraordinarily wholesome element, an enduring inspiration and challenge which I and others, I know, very highly valued.

A much later memory of him, from the time of his retirement in Durham, which I treasure, is of an informal service in the Cathedral arranged by students, which they had invited him to lead and had suggested that I might take part in. While I was of course very much aware of the important contribution he had made to the Anglican Communion and to the World Church, as a theologian and thinker and leader, what struck me again most forcefully was his gentleness and humility, and the fact that one was in the presence of one whom one could without hesitation call 'a man of God'. *(The Revd Professor C. E. B. Cranfield)*

Michael Ramsey—I am sure you will know what a well respected, gentle, man of the people he was. I first met him in 1977. He had asked Canon Douglas Jones, after he returned to live in his beloved Durham, if he could recommend someone to do some typing and I received a letter which I could barely read. I went to meet him, nervously, at his home in South Street and found he was more nervous than I was (I understood that he had worked with more mature secretaries previously!). We had a chat and he handed me several pages of his handwriting which I was to type up and return the following week. I was mortified at having to take the work back with many gaps. I apologised and said something like it was a shame he didn't dictate his work. He was over the moon to find that I knew shorthand and proceeded to dictate the next batch. It was amusing to watch his huge bushy eyebrows moving over the top of his papers as he struggled from time to time to read his own handwriting!

The following year our third child was born and Bishop and Lady Ramsey came to our house for three or four weeks for our sessions. He was quite at home dictating with a tray of coffee and a dog sprawled across his feet while Lady Ramsey was in another room willing a very young baby to wake up and cry so that she could be lifted out. When our daughter started school I returned to work part time in the Theology Department but continued to see him on a weekly basis.

We met one day in the bank in Durham and walked outside together to stand for a short time chatting. Everybody knew him and several were pointing. I said to him, "you know what they were saying—who is that talking to Margaret Parkinson?" He chuckled and laughed to the point of embarrassment before walking with me along Saddler Street.

We worked together for ten years and I was sorry to see him leave Durham. We visited the Ramseys at Bishopthorpe shortly before they moved to Oxford taking a large bag of home grown vegetables, which they loved; and we went to see Lady Ramsey at the nursing home about a year after Bishop Ramsey died. He was a lovely, much missed character. *(Mrs Margaret Parkinson)*

A staunch supporter of St Mary's College was Michael Ramsey, a Canon of the Cathedral at the time of Miss Ferguson's negotiations with the Dean and Chapter about permitting students to walk through The College for access to St Mary's, then using the present Chorister School buildings. He it was who, when the basement room under the East JCR [*Junior Common Room—Editor*] of the New College was the best that could be done to provide a chapel, came in 1952 to dedicate it: "The University Grants Committee made it a rule not to contribute towards the cost of a chapel, but they did not object to the setting aside of a room for the purpose. That good friend of the College, Dr Michael Ramsey, now Archbishop of Canterbury, then Bishop of Durham, came in cope and mitre and with pastoral staff to bless the tiny, crowded chapel".

Bishop Ramsey continued to take a great interest in the College and its affairs, and visited the basement chapel and its larger successor on several other occasions. It is fitting that on his death in 1989 it was decided that a series of Michael Ramsey Memorial Lectures, arranged in conjunction with the Department of Theology and the Dean and Chapter, be instituted to mark the close and happy association between Bishop Ramsey and St Mary's College.

Miss Margaret Beveridge Fergusson was Principal of St Mary's from 1940 to 1955. Most of this information is taken from her (typescript) Reminiscences, c. 1973, in the College Archives. (*Elizabeth B. Boyd*)

My father, Canon N. D. Coleman, was Acting Precentor at the Cathedral during the war and lecturer at the Theology Department. My sister, Phoebe Coleman, and I were very privileged to be present at the wedding in the Galilee Chapel on 8th April 1942, which I recollect was either at 9.30 a.m. or 10.00 a.m., and at the reception given by the Bishop of Jarrow and Mrs Owen where we were very warmly welcomed by Canon Ramsey, as he was then.

A very cherished memory was being invited to Afternoon Tea, just the two of us aged 12 and ten. We were the first visitors they had invited to tea since the wedding and we were impressed by their informality and friendliness. Mrs Ramsey showed us her wedding presents and we particularly remember being shown the linen cupboard and noticing the chapel they had made just inside the front door.

When we left Durham in January 1945, Mrs Ramsey succeeded our mother as the Enrolling Member of St Mary's Mothers' Union. *(Dorothea Neil Smith)*

Michael Ramsey served his first curacy at Our Lady and St Nicholas in Liverpool where he was popular with the ladies of the parish, at least one of whom fancied becoming Mrs Ramsey. They used to darn his socks for him because he was hopeless at anything like that. As curate, he was frequently in the Parish Church School where the headmistress was Miss Florrie, a diminutive lady.

Years later, when he had retired, I was present when he returned to the parish and presided at the Eucharist. Miss Florrie, then aged about 90 and a stalwart of the congregation, brought the Offertory up and the flagon was placed on the altar. Michael Ramsey then leant across the altar and embraced Miss Florrie warmly. How the bread and wine didn't go flying I will never know because all we could see was a tangle of vestments and bodies that was Miss Florrie and Michael Ramsey in an embrace divided by the altar table. *(Dr Paul Laxton)*

Four memories:

1. Being rather daunted as a new Canon by his presence in the Quire as I preached (in those days we preached at a lectern in the middle of the Quire at the main Eucharist). When I told him afterwards he said that he had not heard anything offensive or heretical — yet.

2. He came to my house to meet informally with the first group of students on NEOC *[North East Œcumenical Course — Editor]* and he was interested/ intrigued by the men, in middle age and one older, from a variety of north-east backgrounds (one was a miner from Ashington and I still hear news of him, probably in his 80s). Michael sat in an armchair and they gathered

round him, a bit in awe but also warming to him and the quality of what he had to say.

3. One Sunday morning after the service I was following him through the south transept on his way to the Slype and I heard a woman say to him, "I know you from somewhere but I can't remember who you are". It was too tempting not to eavesdrop, so I hovered and he said, "Well, I used to be the Bishop of Durham..." and she said, "Of course, now I remember." I can't reproduce the rise and fall of that celebrated voice, but it was splendid and, of course, unlike some others who might spring to mind he didn't say "Well, I used to be the Archbishop of Canterbury"!

4. When he came to dedicate the M and S window [*This is the 'Daily Bread' Window' at Durham Cathedral, designed by Mark Angus, funded by Marks and Spencer and dedicated on 2 May 1984—Editor*] he was standing in front of it with Peter Baelz [*then The Dean of Durham—Editor*] and the designer. A member of congregation said loudly and clearly, "Well, it's obscene." I don't think the comment was picked up, but afterwards Peter and Michael did relish that, quite unawares, the remark had been made in the presence of the Artist. If Michael had said anything it might have been, "Really, do you, how very interesting." *(The Revd Canon Ronald Coppin)*

❖   ❖   ❖

I am one of Michael Ramsey's nephews. I have a book that he gave me about the story of Rome, it is inscribed 'Rev. Arthur Michael Ramsey, from Father and Mother. Nov 14th 1915'. That was his 11th birthday.

Inscription by his mother in a book given to Michael Ramsey on his eleventh birthday (courtesy of Mr Michael Barcroft)

He told me this story when I visited him as the newly appointed Headmaster of the Cathedral School in Peterborough.

'When I was a child, my bedroom was one of the attics of our new Edwardian house in Cambridge called 'Howfield'. There was no electricity in the attics and when I went to bed I had to read by candlelight. My bookshelf was in a recess and it was difficult to identify my books by sight. I had been given a series of children's history books, about ten of them, the most familiar being 'Our Island Story'. These became great favourites and I learned to identify each by its individual smell.'

"Well," I replied, "for some reason I have come into possession of one of those history books, inscribed with your name as a gift from your parents in 1915. It is among my books in the Headmaster's study at school. At Speech Day tomorrow, we will be having tea in the study. Why don't we blindfold you and then ask you to smell out the book?"

This was agreed and at the Governors' tea held in the study, the head boy ceremonially blindfolded the Archbishop with a school scarf and I presented him with the book. After a number of hearty sniffs and a deep sigh, the Archbishop pronounced, "Story of Rome". He was right!

We used to send a group every year to Durham to do field studies, he always had them out for an evening to talk about Peterborough.

Once during his retirement he got stuck in the bath and Joan had to call the Cathedral Land Agent (who lived nearby) in the middle of the night to come and get him out.

He enjoyed telling the story of the occasion when he went to preach in Wales. He took his archbishop's kit with him in a suitcase and left it in the foyer of the hotel and, when the car came to collect him to go to the church, picked up the only suitcase in the foyer assuming it was his. When he got to the church it was full of climbing gear—so someone had gone climbing with a suitcase full of archbishop's kit. *(Michael Barcroft)*

We moved to 15 The College when my father became Bishop of Jarrow in 1950 when I was 8 years old. I was often in the Ramseys' house in the short time we coincided as they had no children and were very welcoming — indeed Michael Ramsey asked me to choose one of his books to keep when they were preparing to move to Cambridge, I have it still — a very old Child's Book of Saints.

On the day of their removal we noticed our elderly cat Sheba had gone missing. We feared she had gone on to the riverbanks and fallen foul of the feral cats there. However, we had a phone call from Cambridge to say that when the Ramseys unpacked their furniture van — there was Sheba fast asleep on an arm chair. Considering her age we agreed that she should stay with them. As she didn't come back with them to Auckland I assume she didn't survive the two years in Cambridge. We had progressed on to dogs by then!

I was privileged to be part of the Ramseys' 'family' when he was consecrated and when he was put in to Durham, York and Canterbury. He was a favourite visitor to our house in spite of breaking a chair with his memorable 'sway'! *(Catherine Bartlett née Ramsbotham)*

He was a wonderful teacher and spiritual mentor, with a most alert mind, hilarious wit, and an eager spirit of interest and enquiry. To visit him was to be welcomed by warmth and silence in equal measure. To speak to him in person or by telephone was to sense immediately his kindness and total interest. His greatest gift was to encourage and to impart a sense of joy, which dispelled despondency and any narrowness of vision. Even in the memory this remains potent and true; he fulfilled his own dictum about being a saint — he made God real.

Memory is a powerful thing, and Bishop Michael certainly leaves sense of his presence and character upon it. Many of our conversations occurred walking through the fields around Cuddesdon, or along the river in Durham. There were extraordinary moments such as when he got stuck on a stile and refused to move until he had finished what he was saying; or when he fell into a snow-drift in Durham and lay there laughing and throwing snowballs, and then got up covered in snow to make a point about theology!

He was generous with his time and with his books, never happier than when he could get on with whatever was in hand, while a young student sat lodged in the corner of his study with a volume of the Fathers. He would pace up and down, and then suddenly ask what one was reading and make a pertinent or ironic comment about it, before lapsing back into purposeful silence. He taught as much by his silences as by his words, by his attitude and example as by his advice, which he was often cautious about giving. He was a loving father-in-God, as well as, in the words placed on his memorial at Canterbury Cathedral, a 'scholar, priest and friend'. (*The Revd Douglas Dales, originally published in 'Glory: The Spiritual Theology of Michael Ramsey'*)

Myself and two other boys made up the choir of St Michael and All Angels in Esh Village, the year was 1954, we were aged 12 or 13 years old. Bishop Ramsey paid a visit to the Parish and attended a service at the Church. After the service everyone was invited over the road to have tea and buns at the Church of England School and meet the Bishop—the same Bishop who attended The Queen at Her Coronation and all of us had seen him on television the previous year. ...WOW... Little did I realise that within a few short years I would be escorting The Queen on State occasions, as a Member of The Household Cavalry.

We three boys tucked into sticky buns while the grown ups chatted with the Bishop but after a short while the Bishop walked slowly over to us three warblers with sticky fingers. I remember thinking that he seemed to have walked straight out of a chapter of a book about Christianity in the Middle Ages, a large and jovial man with a bald pate and long white hair and bushy eyebrows. I also remember when he spoke to us those eyebrows would rise and fall with the level of conversation. They fascinated me, but what a warm and friendly man.

Bishop Ramsey is how I think a Bishop and Archbishop should look and sound like, with the common touch. A lovely man. (*Walter Pennick*)

Soon after he became Bishop of Durham he seems to have visited many, perhaps all of the parishes in the Diocese. In the village where I lived, the parish breakfast on the occasion of this visit was held in the local big house and I was so impressed by this large and very friendly man seated on a settee and chatting to everyone, including youngsters like me.

Who of my age can forget the Coronation? As a patriotic 13 year old watching on our neighbours' small television screen I remember my pride at seeing our bishop standing at the Queen's right hand. I often mention this when doing tours and talking about the importance of the Bishops of Durham. I had been confirmed by Michael Ramsey's predecessor the day the King died, so had good reason to remember so vividly. (*Mrs Sylvia Graham*)

I only met Archbishop Michael Ramsey on two occasions in my life; the first was nearly 50 years ago, during my training for the priesthood at The Queen's College, Birmingham, and the second came many years later, during my first Christmas Day in the Diocese of Durham. At Queen's College we always ended each day with the Office of Compline in the college chapel. On Friday evenings the service always included an address, often given by a guest visitor, and on this particular occasion the guest was the Archbishop. He took the theme of worship, and I have never forgotten his words concerning the *Sursum Corda* in the Eucharist. In his gentle and characteristic style of speaking, he encouraged us to think of heaven and earth as coming together when we hear the words …
"therefore with angels and archangels and with all the company of heaven, we laud and magnify thy glorious name." We all felt for a special moment the reality of those words, and sometimes, hopefully often, I have remembered them during the years that have followed.

The other occasion was a chance encounter with Archbishop Michael and his wife after a Christmas morning Eucharist, here in the Cathedral. I had recently come to the diocese as vicar of a parish in South Shields, but on this occasion I was able to bring my elder son to the 11.15 a.m. Eucharist, after our own Parish Eucharist at 9.30 a.m. Stephen had graduated from

Durham University many years previously but was anxious to spend part of his Christmas morning in his beloved cathedral. The Ramseys were amongst the congregation, sitting in the Quire area, and after the service I was able to speak to them, and gratefully reminded Archbishop Michael of his words in the college chapel over 40 years ago. I can't say that he was able to recall the occasion with any great clarity but his joy to be reminded of it was very obvious to my son and myself and showed yet again the gentle graciousness of this remarkable and saintly man. *(The Revd Canon David Couling)*

I met Michael Ramsey when he was visiting Athens for an ecumenical event and had lunch at the British Embassy. The head of the British School of Archaeology, Sinclair Hood, asked him a rather leading question, "What do you think of the theology of the Greek Church?" Ramsey leaned right across the shiny table and said, "Err. Um, er, um, mmm, er, mmm" then eventually said something like, "It's a wonderful church" thus making it clear in a mumbly way that he didn't really want to answer the question. *(Mrs Jasmine Blakeway)*

I had a long acquaintance with the Ramseys as they had been at the wedding of my parents (Brian and Isabel Canning) before the war. They were thus pleased when my father was installed in a parish in Kent when he was Archbishop. After he retired to Durham, Joan and he attended my parent's ruby wedding anniversary celebrations which we held in Collingwood College. My husband and I particularly remember Joan for her interest in our well being and hope that your book will pay tribute to her contribution to his ministry. *(Mrs Mary Gullick)*

We decided to invite Michael and Mrs. Ramsey to our NEOC end of summer school party—knowing that he enjoyed his food, conversation with students and a glass of red wine. As a brand new member of the course I was deputed to call at his house in the Bailey to convey the invitation—which I did with some trepidation. The door was opened by

Mrs Ramsey, whom I told that I had come from NEOC to invite them to a party. My hesitancy (and Yorkshire accent) led to a pronunciation of NEOC that must have been difficult to decipher. She shouted loudly up the stars to Michael saying, "There's someone here come from New York to invite us to a party". He showed neither surprise nor disappointment when he discovered that the party was just across the road at St John's College rather than across the pond in the USA.

At the party one of my fellow students who had become obsessed with the idea that St John's Gospel had been assembled in the wrong order pinned Michael in a corner while he explained his theory in depth his theory. This was an exercise that he had attempted in a New Testament essay that had not been well received by the examiners. Michael, in his ingenious way courteously excused himself saying, "That is a very interesting proposition". Thereafter my fellow student pressed his hypothesis on anyone who had the misfortune to be available, asserting that the Archbishop considered it to be a very interesting proposition. *(Revd David Simon)*

When Michael Ramsey moved back to Durham in retirement he gave a lecture to the University Liberal Club. Stephen Sykes, then Canon Professor, was in the chair and he told a story of how he had met Michael Ramsey at an event at Church House. Ramsey had walked into a glass door, stepped back in surprise, blinked and walked into it again.

When he arrived in the USA on an official visit he disembarked from the liner at the port to be greeted by a phalanx of the press. One of them called out to him, "Archie! Will you be visiting any night clubs while you are in New York?" to which he replied, "Are there any night clubs in New York?" The New York press scrummage resulted in headlines the next day, 'Archbishop's first question: "Are there night-clubs in New York?"'

During his retirement he was a frequent visitor to St Chad's, where he was a member of the SCR. He was warm and friendly, with no small talk, but bursting to life if one mentioned St John or the Holy Spirit. At SCR business meetings he would sit back in an armchair holding up the minutes or agenda paper in front of his face as if totally bewildered—and then come up with a penetrating question. *(Dr Douglas Pocock)*

My husband, Canon Alan Lazonby, was Vicar of Witton Park in the 1950s and combined that with being Domestic Chaplain to Michael Ramsey between about 1953 and 1957. He loved Michael Ramsey and, when Alan was training at St John's, had spent three mornings a week doing various jobs for him. Michael Ramsey christened our daughter and he was absolutely super with the children at the party after the Christening— somewhere I have a photo of him with them in the dining room, they loved his Episcopal cross and ring. He was so fatherly to the children.

He loved his garden at Auckland Castle and would go out in the early morning to smell the roses.

Alan then became Rector of St Andrew's, Haughton le Skerne. When Ramsey was Archbishop of York he and Joan came to tea and it was just like an ordinary couple having afternoon tea. After he left York we continued to receive a Christmas card from them and Alan loved to read anything and everything that Ramsey wrote. When Alan retired from Haughton le Skerne, Archbishop Ramsey came to the leaving party and made a lovely speech.

I remember his bushy eyebrows which went up and down, up and down, up and down. If he was saying something or commenting on something that he didn't quite believe his eyes would twinkle. I have such lovely memories of him. *(Mrs Joan Lazonby)*

Letter from Canon Lazonby to Professor Owen Chadwick

Dear Mr Chadwick,

Thank you for your letter. I hope what I have to say in reply is helpful to your undertaking. I'm typing it because you couldn't read it otherwise, so my wife tells me.

I'm not sure whether it is only Michael Ramsey's years as Bishop of Durham on which you want me to comment. I knew him well before that when he was Professor at Durham and my own theological tutor. Every Saturday morning in term I had an hour with him. I can't say I presumed to get to know him. I always was, and still am, in awe of him. But I do remember his gentleness in criticism of an essay, his quiet piercing the bubble of turgid writing and the way in which he would correct a misstatement so that one thought he had discovered the mistake oneself. I remember once his, "I don't think I would go as far as that" as a comment on part of one essay I wrote where I suggested that Abraham was not necessarily one person but the person arising out of the movement of a tribe.

As for his lectures on theology, it still seems to me they were miracles of concision and clarity, delivered at a pace which made it possible even for those who had no shorthand to get down pretty well verbatim. As I remember, there was little discussion and hardly ever any argument. To us in those far off days of 1941 it was almost as though God himself was speaking.

But, coming to his episcopate, I well remember the incredulity and laughter in the diocese when he turned up in a taxi. He knew he needed to be able to get about the diocese. He had no knowledge of, or interest in cars, did not drive himself and so purchased the nearest thing to what he was used to, namely, the London taxi. It served him well, easy to get in and out of, roomy, reliable, reasonable comfortable so he was able to read on the way to his appointments, but a great source of loss of face for his chauffeur.

He brought a residentiary domestic chaplain with him (I can't remember his name) but that didn't last long. I think he just didn't want to be bothered by having someone under his feet all the time. And I suspect too that at that time he didn't really know what to do with a chaplain. Certainly when he invited me to go part-time, the job turned out to be much less that what I have since gathered later chaplains to other bishops have done (but that may, of course have been my own incapacity).

Of course, I am talking of the time when there was an 'unreformed' Church of England and the style of the episcopate was a very different one from that of today. I remember Michael Ramsey's predecessor, Alwyn Williams, always replied to letters from his clergy by return of post in his own hand. Michael's method was very much the same though he did have most of his letters and papers typed (not an unwise thing in view of his execrable handwriting). He used me largely as a secretary for more personal dealings with his clergy whilst his secretary proper (Mary Ellis RIP) dealt more with diocesan and Anglican matters. I did not accompany him to most institutions and confirmations unless I would have been going anyway. He preferred to appoint a chaplain for the evening on his arrival. I did go to all cathedral 'do's' and the bigger events. We travelled together since at the time I did not have a car of my own. We chatted little. He was not one for small talk. He did, however, regularly quiz me about the diocese and people, not just when travelling but in his study too. I was born, brought up and educated in the Bishopric and prided myself on my knowledge of the area, both Church and State, as it were. So the Bishop would bring up a topic, refer to a place or personage and wait for my reaction. I was nearly always able to make more relevant comment but I often wondered why he had bothered to ask because his response always showed up just how great was his grasp of the situation and how wise and accurate his summing up of the person. I am sure he was helped in this by Joan, his wife, who after all had developed a wide knowledge of the diocese through her work with the Bishop of Jarrow. But there was no doubting Michael's own, almost intuitive, group of things. It was as if he could conduct business simultaneously on two quite different planes. I was on one. He at least could see through to the other where the true realities lay.

People used to say that he looked much older than he was, that he often seemed to be remote (not in an unkindly manner) and, while accepting the godliness and sincerity of the man, questioned his competence as a bishop and therefore, necessarily, an administrator.

I could not agree with this. He took, for example, endless pains over appointments to benefices. One would find lying about in his study old envelopes with lists on the back of vacant parishes or those about to become vacant would be in one column and the names of men who could fill them in another. You could find two or three lists with the same parishes on but different names, or some names crossed out. An Anglo-Catholic himself, he was meticulous in his respect for parochial tradition.

And he thought ahead. Like a good chess player, he always seemed to be planning the third or fourth future move. It didn't always work out as he had planned but I am convinced he did have a plan for the diocese, which unfortunately for us, he was unable to complete.

He agonised about the quality of the ministry. I remember going into his study one morning to find him, not sitting at his desk or in his favourite chair, but striding up and down with a face like thunder and brandishing a letter from someone outside the diocese, whose name had been suggested to him during one if his forays to London. The curate, in the offending letter, was declining the offer. That in itself didn't matter. The reason he gave did, very much. He declined because he said, "working in such a situation would be unworthy of his talents". I wrote the reply. It was brief and two-edged. "Dear ...., Thank you for our letter. I note your refusal and reason. Yours sincerely." Michael was truly incensed at this slight to the people whom he served and truly loved. I never saw him so angry at any other time.

He could be naughty. I remember Mary Ellis, his secretarys buttonholing me when I went into Auckland Castle one morning when the Ramseys were away on holiday. The staff had decided to clean the study while he was safely out of the way. Under the loose cushion of his chair they had found several letters, all of them presenting awkward problems upon which he was, literally, sitting. The letters were placed in the pending file. By the time the bishop returned several problems had resolved themselves. I can't help wondering what would have happened if there had been no spring cleaning.

His other worldliness was real, but only one side of him. Those keen eyes under beetling brows missed nothing. And he remembered people too. Leslie Lawrence was vicar of a church in Jarrow but left for somewhere near Wakefield a couple of months after Michael was consecrated. Previously Leslie had been an itinerant Church Army Captain and so had had no contact with the Bishop when he was a Professor at Durham. A week before Leslie left there was a Confirmation in the old church at Jarrow and he was presenting some candidates from his parish. When the clergy had robed, they moved to the vestry where the Bishop was and he had a word with each one. Leslie told him he was off to Wakefield in the next few days.

One of the Bishop's first engagements, when in 1956 he went to York as Archbishop, was to address the Wakefield Diocesan Conference. This was held in some place where the entrance to the hall was at the top of a wide staircase. Leslie told me, when we met a month or two afterwards at a TA Chaplains' Conference that he was ascending this staircase when from behind him there came a voice at the foot of the stairs, "Wait a minute, Lawrence! I want a word with you". It was the Archbishop, whom he had met briefly only once but who had not only remembered the meeting but the name of the man involved, and that from the rear.

I remember too that my second daughter was born at Witton Park when I was chaplain and the Bishop came to baptise her. Afterwards, after tea, my son, aged seven and two or three other little boys clustered round the Bishop asking him the usual questions of, "What's this?" and, "Why do you wear that?" I vividly remember the courtesy and, I believe, the enjoyment he showed as he dealt with their query even to the extent of allowing at least one to climb on his knee the better to see his pectoral cross.

It would be true, I think, to say that he was not entirely at ease with casual acquaintances and could not enter into the mundane conversation which marks the relationships of so many of us. Small talk for him was more that of the Senior Common Room than of the fireside. And yet, because of the charisma (I didn't want to use that word but there really in no other) of the man he was accepted by all and all were grateful for his presence in their gatherings, whatever they were. The people of Bishop Auckland used to love it when their Bishop was seen in Woolworths. Whether he ever bought anything, I was never told.

His sense of humour was not always apparent. I remember he took great delight in telling people what the favourite hymn of the Archbishop of Cape Town. "Joost as I am". And I think the same impish humour was lurking there, though there was a serious intent as well, when, at the unveiling of his portrait in Auckland Castle he said that, no matter what he did or who he had been, in the end it wouldn't matter. He wasn't greatly bothered about the opinion of posterity. Posterity will, I'm sure, have a different idea.

I hope whcat I have written, even if in itself unusable, will help you to a better understanding of one who both gave and merited and gained love.

Yours sincerely
Alan Lazonby

P.S. He thought you should have been Bishop of Durham after him. I remember his disappointment when he learned that the letter to you had crossed in the post with your acceptance of the Mastership of Selwyn.

Dr Wilfred Chapman was Bishop Ramsey's GP until he retired and then I took over. I only saw him on a couple of occasions, once after a minor traffic accident at Leazes Bowl roundabout in which he hit his head. He was taken to Dryburn Hospital where he was examined, X-rayed and sent home. I visited him later that week with the X-ray results. Lady Ramsey asked me, "What did the X-ray show?" I relied that there was nothing there to which she replied, "I have long suspected that." (*Dr Philip Tattersall*)

A student informed Michael that he chose to be a humanist (presumably rather than a Christian). Michael replied that he chose to be a Christian humanist. I have tried to follow Michael's example in this, accepting and using positive attitudes rather than try to demolish them. I like to think that I too am a Christian humanist. (*A member of the diocesan clergy*)

Bishop Ramsey, as he and I agreed I would call him in a professional context, had no small talk. At drinks parties—which everyone thought they should invite him to—people flocked round him at the start but as the evening wore on they gradually backed off leaving him on his own.

The Ramseys had two ladies to look after them. The first, Miss Tankery, also looked after the small boarding house that then existed at the High

School. She went to York with them. When they came back they had a very peculiar lady who loved mice and kept funny dogs. She moved with them from South Street to the Bailey. You could get landed with her at social events. I don't think Lady Ramsey, who looked rather like the film star Jessie Matthews, did much housekeeping.

Bishop Ramsey used to walk in the middle of the road, his mind far away on other things. Once we were in Upper Teesdale at the top of Caldron Snout and we saw a lone figure among a field of stacked hay. When we got closer we realised it was Bishop Ramsey. He obviously liked walking in fields and always looked as though he was in communion with a pile of hay.

In retirement he said the only place he would like to be apart from Durham was Chicago. I can't think why he wanted to go there. He was very impressed with the grass there. [*I think 'Chicago' may have been his shorthand for Nashotah House in Wisconsin, one hundred miles away   That is in open countryside. Editor*] (*A Durham Resident*)

Michael Ramsey, Bishop of Durham in the 1950s could be seen walking in Newgate Street, Bishop Auckland every Thursday morning. The street in those days was very busy with double decker buses and cars etc. running up the main street. Lots of people would be milling about on market day but he stood out in the crowd in his black garb and gaiters. He always had a pleasant half smile on his face. My friend and I always looked out for the sight of him on our Thursday morning shopping trips as he made his way about the town. I am now 85 years old and still remember those days quite well. (*Mrs Elizabeth Sayers*)

The only little story I have to offer is from my visit to him in retirement in Durham on 15 March 1983 when I went to see him to do a taped interview about the centenary history of the Community of the Resurrection which I was just beginning to research. As you know Michael was awkward at greetings and goodbyes. As we came down the stairs there was a very scruffy hot water bottle in a stained and dilapidated knitted jacket at the foot of the stairs. He said to me, "is that your hot water bottle?" This is a rather trivial story but does illustrate his awkwardness in relating to people and possibly his quirky sense of humour. *(The Revd Canon Alan Wilkinson)*

I have a very touching memory of Bishop Ramsay, which I recall with real affection. As you will gather from the photocopied letter and the envelope, I wrote to the Bishop at his Durham address in 1979. I was considering whether I, brought up as a Methodist but worshipping at St Johns', Neville's Cross, should be confirmed with my two young daughters who were preparing for confirmation. You can imagine how surprised I was to receive a personal letter from the Bishop, posted in Japan!

'Thank you for your letter which has been forwarded to us on a visit to Japan. I have read your letter with sympathy. I now hold no office in the church and can give no authoritative guidance. I can only describe to you what is the teaching and practice of the Anglican Church.

We welcome to communion non-Conformists who are communicant members of their own church. But if they wish to share regularly to commune with us and be members of the Anglican Church, it is expected that they will be confirmed: and confirmation is itself a great means of grace.

I hope this makes the position clear and you may feel drawn to be confirmed like your daughters.

+ Michael Ramsey
P.S. Confirmation is not a kind of imposition. It is a means of blessing.'

I'm sure you will agree with me that his response was just as indicative of his true stature as when he took part in the Coronation of Queen Elizabeth II. I totally support the words in the newspaper article ,"approachable, unassuming and with great affection", as a very human person.

I thank everyone taking part in these acts of remembrance and look forward to the unveiling of his memorial window and the publication of your book. *(Mrs Barbara McFarlane)*

A letter about confirmation from Bishop Michael Ramsey to Mrs Barbara McFarlane (courtesy of Mrs Barbara McFarlane)

The last time I saw Michael Ramsey in Durham was shortly after my nephew Andrew was confirmed and I was back in the north-east for the Confirmation service, now more than 25 years ago. He was walking down South Bailey when I encountered the great and saintly man—dressed not in cope and mitre but in plastic packamac and waterproof pork-pie hat. His sight was failing badly and he wore spectacles with very thick lenses. I engaged in a brief conversation telling him of the confirmation the previous evening. He replied with a triple, "Wonderful". Thereafter he trotted off down the street swaying from side to side and swinging his walking stick round and round in the same manner as Charlie Chaplin used to in the old black and white films. My final view of one of God's 20th Century saints. *(Father David Reynish)*

In the summer of 1955, Canon Eric Symes Abbott, Dean of King's College, London (later Dean of Westminster), invited some of his end of first year students to spend a study week at Hawarden Library in North Wales. At dinner with us on the first evening was the Bishop of Durham, the Rt Revd Arthur Michael Ramsey. At the end of the meal there was a bit of banter going on and the Bishop joined in. With a big grin on his face and eyebrows waving, he asked, "Do you know the motto of the dentist?". No-one knew. He said, "It is in the Psalms, 'Open thy mouth wide and I shall fill it'". He was delighted with the response to his joke, and he roared with laughter.

On the occasion of the Memorial Service for our Bishop, the Rt Revd Ian Thomas Ramsey, the Archbishop of Canterbury, the Most Revd Arthur Michael Ramsey, was present in the Cathedral. We clergy were sitting at the front of the nave, on both sides. At the end of the service the procession set off as usual, but the Archbishop stopped on the top step of the Chancel. Robed as he was in cope and mitre, he appeared to fill the opening in the screen. He stood and looked at us all, moving his head from side to side to miss nobody, eyebrows waving. I thought, "He is Gandalf!". That is how powerful his presence was, and how empowering his personality. *(The Revd Sam Burrows)*

About Lord Ramsey—Around 1960—65 or so I took my mother to Hovingham, the home of the Worseley Family, where the daughter was holding her marriage reception after being married by the Canon in York Minster. Memory fails to give me either her first name or the name of her husband who I think was a son of the Duke of Kent. But they all drove up and climbed up the front steps to the main entrance, every one looking before them with determination except Canon Ramsey, who gracefully turned around, smiling and waving to the waiting crowd who had been waiting for some long time. Great man…..memorable. *(Cordeline Stamp)*

Like many other people, I enjoyed seeing Michael Ramsey from time to time when he came back to live in Durham. I was a member of a local group,' The Quick and the Dead', named after Canon Oliver Quick, formerly of the Cathedral clergy before he went to an appointment in Oxford. Two of the founder members were Canon Luce, at that time Headmaster of Durham School, and Dr John R McDonald, a much-liked medical practitioner in the city. When the group met it was often in one another's houses.

Bishop Ramsey, as he liked to be known, accepted an invitation to rejoin this society. I remember how excited he was when shown the notebook containing the minutes of the meetings he had attended in the past. The subject on which he chose to speak was 'The Future of the House of Lords.' It was not only the contents of his talk that appealed to me so memorably but the way he read it—his points of emphasis, his deliberate hesitations, and his facial expressions. Producing a paper with notes for a speech he had made in the Lords at a time when the ordination of women was a current issue, he said he was going to quote from a hymn that was not often sung—'There is a room for new creation in the Upper House of Bliss.' He had hardly finished before there was a roar of delighted approval from us all. *(Roger Till)*

In the 1940s, I was at school in Durham. Every month in term time we attended Choral Evensong in the Cathedral and I have a clear memory of hearing Canon Ramsey reading the first lesson on Advent Sunday—the call of Isaiah. He impressed me as a benign old gentleman with a strange but remarkably clear voice. I didn't realise at the time that he was comparatively young.

After National Service I went up to Cambridge and was somewhat surprised in my first week up there to see Canon Ramsey belting along King's Parade on his bicycle, white hair streaming in the wind behind him. He was then Regius Professor of Divinity.

I was going through the anti-church phase at the time, but some friends persuaded me to accompany them to Great St Mary's Church where Professor Ramsey was preaching. This sermon really was a brilliant piece of work—couched in language simple enough for anyone to understand but full of food for thought enough to challenge much sharper intellects than mine. Professor Ramsey's text was Eph 6:12—years before the Burgess—McLean scandal exploded. Soon afterwards Professor Ramsey became Bishop of Durham. *(Harold Addison)*

While I was Chaplain at Imperial College, South Kensington, I invited Archbishop Ramsey to conduct a Mission for a week. During the week he came to give lectures to hundreds of science and engineering students in vast lecture theatres, followed by invigorating question and answer sessions. One afternoon he arrived, emerging in his purple cassock from the famous Morris Minor he used in London. He entered the large foyer of the Mechanical Engineering Department—where a simple table had been set up as an altar, just a few feet away from a large turbine installation and surrounded by hundreds of students and staff—and celebrated the Eucharist. Students loved him and hung upon his every word.

There are many stories to be told. After one of his lectures, in a question and answer session, I well remember a perplexed 20 year old engineer expressing his confusion about faith to the Archbishop and asking, "Archbishop, what should I believe?" After a moment's quiet Archbishop Ramsey said to the young man, "Be true to that which is deepest within you. Yes! Yes!" To another who asked, "What is the core of the gospel?" he replied succinctly, "Sacrificial love, sacrificial love". Another asked, "What do you think of Jehovah's Witnesses, Archbishop?" After a long silence, and puckering his eyebrows, he naughtily replied, "I don't think about them! I don't think about them! Yes! Yes!"

I loved Archbishop Ramsey and am a better man for being allowed his warm friendship. I thank God for him upon every remembrance. *(The Revd Canon Ivor Smith-Cameron)*

When there was a great protest against the Vicar of Tyne Dock and his congregation over very 'high church' practices *[A very difficult situation which Ramsey inherited in which conciliation failed and the case ran for several more years—see Chadwick p83— Editor]* Ramsey was reported to have said that, "These dear people are simply trying to worship God." *(The Revd Canon Richard Davison)*

Before John Robinson published 'Honest to God', he sent a copy to Archbishop Ramsey for his appraisal. He heard nothing from him so after some time he published it. Michael Ramsey was not pleased and said he should have been consulted only to find the copy John Robinson had sent him down the side of his settee. I do not know who told me this anecdote many years ago but it was believed to be authentic. *(Revd Dorothy Wilson)*

I only saw him the once when, one weekday around 1974, I was in Durham, between Bimbis and Woolworths. I noticed an elderly gentleman walking quite briskly down Silver Street: partly-bald, clad in grey if I remember correctly. I had seen him before but couldn't place him. Later I realised it was Dr Ramsey who I'd seen on television on Christian and State occasions. He just seemed an unassuming elderly gentleman going about his business. He was by no means doddery and certainly didn't have an air of self-importance. I was quite pleased to hear from people that we had a celebrity living in Durham though he didn't act as if he was one when I saw him. *(Philip Champion)*

Michael Ramsey was standing in the cloisters at the Cathedral when he was told of the appointment of the new Bishop of Durham. He shook his head and said, "It mustn't happen again. It mustn't happen again."

A lady accosted Michael and asked him if he had been saved. He replied, "Madam, I have been saved, I am saved and I live in hope that I shall be saved".

When you met him he might sit for ages before saying anything, but somehow there was a sense of companionship and acceptance which was certainly not always apparent in his successors. I had been ordained Deacon just a week before Michael was consecrated in York Minster and I was one of the many Diocesan clergy who went to the ceremony. That was at Michaelmas in 1952. He ordained me priest in 1953. In the early years when I was the only curate in the Deanery I was often required to act as his chaplain when he visited the Deanery. Joan always used to give strict instruction to make sure the 'tails' on his mitre were straight.

He had a wonderful way of conveying messages from Joan. On one occasion when I went to see him in Lambeth Palace he said, "My wife says I must not forget to ask after your wife." The occasion was when I was invited to consider a job in London, among a number of invitations to move to other work. Michael was incredible in that he always seemed to have time to give and to help resolve just what I ought to do. This was some years after he left the Diocese, but he remembered us and was a source of considerable wisdom and advice.

After he retired and was living in Durham he would sometimes come to the village parish where I was Rector (our son used to go and collect him) and take a part in whatever we were celebrating at that time. For all he was such an important person, he had a willingness to take part in our very ordinary village worship. Other bishops have an air of self-importance, but Michael had a simple humility which endeared him to the ordinary congregations. We have some very special memories of him. *(A member of the Diocesan Clergy)*

Canon Ron Corker used to tell the story of how, when his wife was ill and they needed a holiday, just two days later a cheque arrived from Michael Ramsey. It was amazing how he kept in touch with what was going on with the clergy of the diocese. *(The Revd Stan Buyers)*

I was an undergraduate at St Chad's from 1982—85. My memories of the Ramseys' time in Durham include:

Attending meetings in their house on the Bailey for prospective ordinands, drinking in the holiness (as well as Lady Joan's tea) as we all listened to Bishop Michael talking about priesthood and ordination;

As a member of the JCR executive, attending the 80th birthday party for Bishop Michael in college, thrown by the Principal—and then with a couple of other students helping the Ramseys home (a little unsteady on their feet...) afterwards;

Having the enormous privilege of being amongst those who served for Bishop Michael at Low Mass in the college chapel (and therefore, when serving, then also having the pleasure of escorting both Ramseys into breakfast after the service);

Recalling these instances as part of ordination training at Ridley Hall in the 1990s, as well as the following (extracted from the first page my now ageing MA dissertation):

Chapter One: Introduction

'You're at St. Chad's aren't you? Are you going to London?'

I came out of my daydream and discovered Bishop Michael Ramsey standing next to me on the station platform. Now long retired, he was once again living in Durham where he had at different times been both Professor and Bishop. I had met him occasionally when he had presided at the early morning college Eucharist, and he had recently addressed the University Vocations group, to which I belonged. However I was surprised that he had placed me that frosty February morning, and still more that he had chosen not to keep himself to himself for the three-hour journey. For the young student what followed was an engaging time spent discussing vocation and ordination, the importance of stillness and silence in prayer, and the need for different parties in the Church to pull together, not apart.

The journey was unforgettable for other reasons. Ramsey insisted, despite his frailty, on negotiating the long corridors that led to the buffet car of the swaying Inter City 125, returning almost half an hour later with two tepid, half-full cups of tea and a packet of broken biscuits. Later, eyes shut, he smiled as the person sitting opposite leaned forward to ask me in a loud whisper whether this really was the Archbishop and to comment on how old he was looking was these days. On arrival at London King's Cross, Ramsey refused help with his own baggage and, because I was travelling home to recuperate from illness, he also tried to carry some of mine. We were unsurprisingly the last to reach the end of the platform where my father was waiting to meet me. During the introductions Ramsey quickly recalled licensing him as a parish priest in the Archdiocese of Canterbury some 15 years earlier.

Many others have similar stories to tell, often as inconsequential as mine but always as clearly remembered. All these years after his death (and four Archbishops of Canterbury later) Michael Ramsey continues to be held in high regard and remembered with great personal affection. My interest could have ended with a personal nice story, but my encounters with him during my time in Durham assumed greater significance when, as an ordinand, I began to look more closely at my personal pastoral cycle and faith history.

Michael Ramsey had a huge impact on my ordination training—a supervision with Owen Chadwick helped too!—and consequently continues to make an impression on my ministry today. The accounts of the Transfiguration (especially in Luke) have always fascinated me. (*The Revd Chris Hollingshurst*)

The late New Testament scholar Reginald H. Fuller (1915-2007) who met Bishop Ramsey a number of times had an interesting tale of his period as Bishop of Durham. His widow recalls hearing this one many times.

On a summer evening when it was still light the Bishop, strolling the grounds of the cathedral, met a group of Americans. They regretted that they were unable to tour the cathedral as visiting hours were over. The bishop unlocked one of the doors. They were instructed to look around and the bishop would meet them at the same door in an hour. He forgot about them and they were locked in the cathedral overnight until the staff unlocked the doors the following morning. *(Dr R. Lewis Wright)*

Thursday, 26th January 1978: I was at St Chad's College and Chairman of the University Liberal Club when Michael Ramsey spoke to a very well attended open meeting of the Club in one of the large Elvet Riverside Lecture rooms. *[It was not a meeting of the University Students Union as stated in Professor Owen Chadwick's biography on p.66 — Editor]* The lecture was entitled 'Christianity and Politics'. He described the Church of England as, "a sort of perpetual Lib-Lab pact between the two schools of thought."

I also recall him dealing forcefully with a question about Enoch Powell's call for religion and politics to be separate on the basis that Jesus said that, "My kingdom is not of this world". He became quite animated and corrected Powell's understanding of New Testament Greek. (I think that Powell was appointed to a chair in Greek at Durham before the 1945 election but that he never took up the appointment due to his election to the Commons.) The correct translation, said Michael Ramsey, was, "My kingship is not of this world" and that Christians therefore had the duty of extending his rule in the world which necessitated political involvement. I have always remembered that.

In a letter to me dated 29th January he wrote, "I greatly enjoyed the meeting of the Liberal Society with the other societies last week, and thanks to your planning it was a delightful occasion of meeting together and of discussion after the lecture." *(The Revd Paul Hunt)*

Ramsey stories. They are LEGION! I even came across some when I went to lecture to the Army Chaplains. From Boston, Lincs, my two favourites are these. He was returning to his digs and rang the door-bell; a voice from upstairs opened the window and said, "Mr Ramsey is out", and Michael went away. The other I told him and Joan on one of his return visits to Lincoln. "An old lady is supposed to have helped you across the street when you were only in your 30s." "No, no, no, no," he replied, eyebrows going up and down. Whereupon Joan interjected, "Of course she did, dear, and you didn't notice."

His Transfiguration book, which I know was a favourite of his (Owen Chadwick told me this) was probably the book I relied on most in a successful four-year fight with leukaemia. My book 'Rooted in Detachment' *(Published by Dartman, Longman and Todd* 2007) was inspired by it and the sub-title, 'Living the Transfiguration' is a quotation from AMR. I took a very different approach, going through each of the synoptic narratives, and also taking hold of authors from the past, in a kind of reception-history mode. I also wove into it some of my experiences of illness. The final chapter was inspired by Michael—without any doubt. Sometimes he is, I think, misunderstood in relation to the cross. There are those who regard his Johannine approach to theology as playing down the unreconciled world, epitomised in the cross. But this is not supported by the evidence—not least his attachment to the Lucan narrative, an Anglican trait that goes back to John Hackett in the 17th century.

When I wrote the little book 'Watching and Waiting' (Canterbury Press 2008) on the Advent Antiphons, I decided to us a quotation from Michael's Transfiguration book right at the end, about dying and the afterlife—which for me could have been a reality several times during the illness.

The other side of Michael that may interest was his commitment to something Durham has intermittently supported over the years—the Anglican-Lutheran (especially Nordic) scene. It was through the Anglo-Scandinavian Theological Conferences that Michael gained a great deal, describing the experience as 'theological fun'. Michael wrote to me about the effect of this on him. Michael knew my Danish grandfather, who was

Bishop of Aarhus from 1940-61 and had already met Regin Prenter, the Luther Scholar who my grandfather helped to be the first Professor of Dogmatics at the new Faculty in Aarhus after the War, when he spent a term at Lincoln Theological College. My grandfather's favourite story was in Durham at one of those conferences in the days when you left your shoes outside the bedroom to be polished overnight. The next morning, Regin Prenter came down to breakfast in a state, because the shoes left outside for him were far, far too large (he was a small man); "Why are you so worried?" the others asked; "Because if I have shoes that are far too large, it must mean that someone else has shoes that are far, far too small." The English team knew exactly what had happened, and laughed their heads off. "Oh, yes, it's Ramsey again—and he's gone off for a walk, and he won't have noticed or felt a thing." The Danish bishops—in a country prone to nicknames—called him thereafter 'the shoe-thief.'

The Theological Colleges' Staff Conference was held at Queen's Birmingham at the New Year 1976. The apogee was a presentation on a Pastoral Education Report by Peter Baelz—who did a masterly performance, adroit, detached, keeping to the important issues. But he brought the house down when he told us that, on showing the report to Michael Ramsey, the reaction was: "The best thing you can do with ordinands, with ordinands, with ordinands, is to leave them alone, leave them alone, leave them alone." I've used that on a number of occasions. Of course it's an exaggeration, but it put me in mind of that wonderful passage Dorothy L Sayers' 'The Man Born to be King', where she describes, in the most unsentimental manner, Jesus slowly growing from childhood into adulthood, with God secretly at work in him. It tallied with Cicely Saunders telling us at college, "You clergy really mustn't think you've always got to be around when God is doing his bit."

I recall a conversation with AMR about theology when I said to him, "Well, I'm only an historian." And he replied, "Ah yes, ah yes, ah yes, but as an historian, as an historian, you watch things happen, you watch things happen, yes, you watch things happen." I don't think he realised how motivating that remark was for a young priest in my circumstances, trying to make sense of his vocation.

Then there's David Wilcox's favourite from his Cuddesdon retirement days. "You have modular education here, yes modular education, modular, modular, yes modular education. If I had had modular education, I think I might have got somewhere."

I remember a spell-bindingly simple and profound sermon he preached on a return visit to Boston on the foot-washing.

As David Edwards said at the end of his obituary—"He was loved." *(The Rt Revd Kenneth Stevenson)*

I asked American friends who were staying with me whether they would like to see a play called 'Murder in the Cathedral' which was being performed in Durham Cathedral that evening. One asked whether it was by Agatha Christie! I explained. The performance was in the Galilee Chapel and to my delight Michael Ramsey was sitting next to me. I whispered to my friends that here was a real Archbishop of Canterbury. They were duly impressed. Michael Ramsey chunted to himself throughout the performance and stood up to applaud at the end—so everyone else stood up. *(Lilian Groves)*

I was an ordinand in the York arch-diocese when he was at York and used to go to see him at Bishopthorpe both for interviews and for his gatherings for ordinands. I can still remember the outlines of a masterly little talk in chapel on the combination of grace and human effort in Philippians (2:12-13) and his handling of questions: e.g. on the nuclear weapons 'The argument for deterrence is a decreasingly strong argument'—he had just come back from Russia and visiting Orthodox leaders and he pointed to an oil painting to make the point about the Orthodox and tradition "Even the small corner at the bottom of the picture is part of the whole and must be maintained"—so, to lose that was to lose the whole. From that time I still have a letter written in his own hand, when I decided against a curacy at Beverley Minster which he had proposed, to go to Canon Cecil Bewes at Tonbridge: a most generous letter wishing me well considering that his advice had been rejected!

In his period at the White House, South Bailey, opposite Cranmer Hall where I had been Warden (1970-79), he got wind of the fact that I was then writing a short college history of St John's, 'A College Remembered', printed in 1981. He asked me to lunch during this process, a very pleasant occasion with him and Lady Ramsey—over coffee and out of the blue he suddenly shot the question, from under beetling brows and penetrating gaze, "What do you think is the difference between when you trained and now that you have been training other ordinands?" I found this a poser and took some time to get my bearings! In the end, I said that, when I was training in Cambridge in 1958-60, we were largely expected to be able to make the connections between our theology and pastoral practice—we provided the 'eyes to the hooks' or visa versa: whereas during my time in Cranmer in the 1970s there was an unending cry for relevance: we were expected as staff to justify why we taught what we did and what if any relevance it had to parochial ministry! Michael later reviewed my history in 'Churchman', whose review editor was then Ian Cundy, also a Warden and until recently Bishop of Peterborough, sadly now deceased—again AMR was very generous not least because (as a fellow member of Magdalene College, Cambridge) I had omitted from his cv in the history the period as Regius Professor at Cambridge. When the college prepared special rooms for him from the original monastic foundation, so to my shame I had moved him from the chair in Durham straight to the Diocese without this essential interlude, which I suspect he would have loved to have continued (and I know his teaching in the Cambridge faculty was regarded by many as a highlight). It was, I think, sheer duty and Christian obedience which led him to accept what he called the life of a 'church leader'. Bishop Bengt Sundkler once enthused to me about Michael's appearance at an ecumenical gathering in his Episcopal cassock and how much presence he had, which I also remember when attending a debate in the House of Lords on abortion, which both he and Ian Ramsey (by then his successor) contributed to. In that case I had the sense that the whole house was waiting for Michael to pronounce on the subject—he and Lady Summerskill and Donald Soper all made memorable speeches.

I almost know the addresses in 'The Christian Priest Today' off by heart and don't forget his inspired choice of text for his enthronement in Canterbury Cathedral. 'There went out with him a band of men whose heart the Lord had touched'—I have always felt about him that he had something of the religious genius about him and this showed it. *(The Revd Dr Timothy Yates)*

Looking back, it seems Bishop Michael was always around—maybe he was, I do know he was on good terms with our vicar Hugh Corden and that's why he visited us at Stanley so often. Stanley was in the Chester-le-Street Deanery.

I enclose the booklet for the Pilgrimage to Holy Island on 20th July 1955. The Annual Pilgrimage was always attended by Bishop Michael and the picture *[in 'Tomorrow is born today' by Dewi Morgan, SPG Book of the year 1955-56 published by SPG—Editor]* opposite page 32 shows the walk to Holy Island. I am somewhere just behind the banner.

I think I mentioned this wonderful memory and on various occasions he asked, "Oh—you are one of Corden's girls?" Another time, he asked, "Are you still at Stanley?" Much later, at Lanchester, Canon Chase's 40th Anniversary in 1980, he exclaimed, "So this is where you are!" and in 1981, at the RCM Centenary he remembered me and also asked after my father (Stan Henson) whom he confirmed as an adult (obviously) in 1955. On another occasion, we were meeting my father from the train and Bishop Michael was there too and he remembered my mother had died and mentioned this. He really seemed to have an inbuilt computer—although I would say it was a real gift.

He came to consecrate the newly built St Stephen's at South Stanley. I was in the choir at St Andrews, and we walked/processed all the way. It was a lovely day, June 1954, a bit blowy—I did have a picture of some of us, holding onto our Juliet Caps. *(Mrs Elizabeth Wharton)*

In the autumn of 1952 my father became a Lay Reader and after the service we were invited to tea in the castle—it was there that I first met the Bishop of Durham; he met the families and friends of the new Lay Readers. I was 15 at that time and overawed by the happenings; the Bishop moved round the hall and talked with each group of people and greeted us with a broad smile and we felt his genuine interest and care in the way he talked. He was also well known for spending time talking to young people who he confirmed.

Two and a half years later the Bishop launched a scheme to ordain men who had served the Church in many ways but who could bring a wealth of experience and talents to the sacred ministry of priesthood. This was a very forward looking step and it was successful. My father was accepted for training and was a student in Queen's College, Birmingham. During his year of studies, the Bishop was enthroned in York Minster as Archbishop. He sent two tickets to the college and my father and a friend went to the service, they had reserved seats and afterwards the Archbishop came and spoke to the five men who were waiting to be ordained as deacons. Prior to my father's ordination as deacon, the following year a cheque arrived at our home, this meant a great deal to us. His caring and thoughtful qualities towards people he met in his daily work showed his true calling as a priest. Years later we met and chatted with him after the 11.30 a.m. Holy Communion Service in the Cathedral. I remember his amazing memory for people and his ability to pick up where he had left off when speaking to them.

My family are very thankful for all the help we received from him; his support at this special time was greatly valued. *(Margaret Rushford)*

As Bishop Michael Ramsey's Chaplain for his last months in York and then in Canterbury before I was made his senior Chaplain (October 1960-65; 1965—late 69), I am thrilled at the 'likeness' I discern of Michael in the Window.

I remember one or two things he or Joan told me…

At Auckland Castle he had a barber called Ellis. The way he would cut Michael's hair would leave a discernible ridge at the back, (which he would never notice but which Joan did, and didn't like). Michael referred to it as the 'Ellis Ridge'.

Before his marriage to Joan Hamilton, he had a housekeeper who was punctilious with her absent-minded professor/canon/employer about being paid promptly and properly. "Money lightens labour", she would observe to him.

Another Canon had a limp which Michael greatly admired, and imitated. So the two in procession would limp. Walking one day he noticed he had a real limp until he realised he had been walking with one foot on the pavement and the other in the gutter.

He would never bother to untie his shoes: he would force and struggle until he had bent the heels of his shoes in, to slip his feet into them, and then half heartedly try to pull the heel out from the other.

He used Durhamisms with Joan: the word 'clart' means to talk loudly, complain, I understand. His (cheap, large) alarm clock on his bedside table was known as 'The Clarter'. And he would use this term about certain of his clergy who talked too much.

He loved hock: and beer. One day in my club in London (The St James' Club on Piccadilly) when he came to lunch with me he dismayed John, our dignified and pompous butler, by telling him that he would love a pint of beer not a cocktail. John's face dropped. He recovered and returned with a magnificent Georgian Silver tankard from the Silver Room, which Michael seized and quaffed in front of him: straight down and then asked for another, saying to me meanwhile, "It's no good unless you can have a lot!"

He was the only man I've ever known who on coming into church in the processional hymn 'We love the place, O God,' would be heard singing loudly, 'Turn back, O man...'

Bishop Michael was my Dad. He and Joan would tell their friends that I was the son they never had. I adored them. I wasn't bright enough to be scared of him, and I would (like Joan) argue with him, which he wasn't used to. "Darling," Joan would say, "John's only trying to tell you something you don't want to hear." I travelled with him (and Joan) all over the world. I never laughed more in my life than in that decade. Happy, hilarious laughter. I made him laugh, all the time.

There was one hilarious episode: Christmas Day 1960. I chaplained him into the Minster at York for Matins at 10.00 a.m. before the Great Eucharist (at the High Altar) at 11.00 a.m. The Nave was packed. He came up in rochet and chimere with train (Primates did that, in those days) to the Nave Throne. Two diminutive choristers followed him carrying his train. They arranged it as he sat in his Throne; I sat about four feet away. During Dean Eric Milner-White's sermon I heard fidgeting and a struggle from the Throne.

"What is the matter"?
"I've got my buckle shoes trapped under the rug beneath my chair!"
"How?"
"I don't know, but I can't move".

So on hands and knees and in front of 2000 people in that nave I crawled on my hands and knees, blue Coronation Mantle on, to try to unfasten the buckles trapped under the edge of the rug.....

"You're hurting!"
"It's you're own fault. If you want me to free you I have to tug....."

I struggled, and got his feet free and crawled back. He had a long fit of the giggles. The congregation saw it all. The Dean preached on........

Bishop Michael was a saint, and I knew him at his *nastiest*. *(The Revd Canon John Andrew)*

Newspaper cutting from 'The Sunderland Echo', Saturday, 23rd June, 1962 : 'Visiting the Primate'

'A pair of inlaid book-ends and a walking stick in the shape of a shepherd's crook were the gifts taken by a party of Sunderland Shipyard workers when they set off last night to visit the Archbishop of Canterbury (Dr A. M. Ramsey).

Made by Mr Thomas Banks, a chargeman-joiner at Doxford's Yard, the walking stick is made from walnut with the handle carved from lignium vitae and the book-ends, in the shape of bibles, are walnut, inlaid with teak and white sycamore.

The party which is going to Canterbury at the invitation of the Archbishop, set off from St Luke's Church and was due to arrive at Canterbury in time for breakfast.

The shipyard workers' long association with Dr Ramsey began when he was Bishop of Durham. After visiting Wear Shipyards, Dr Ramsey invited a party of men to Auckland Castle. The men later visited him at Bishopthorpe when he became Archbishop of York.

Most of the 35 men in the party were from Doxford's and Short's but there were others from Austin and Pickersgill's and Bartram's. Alderman J. Tweddle also travelled with the party.' (Sunderland Echo, Saturday, 23rd June, 1962. *(Press cutting supplied by Denis Trigg)*

The visit of Sunderland Shipyard Workers
(courtesy of Mr Denis Trigg)

I was at Durham (St Chad's, 1945—48). During a month in term-time, when Michael Ramsey was Canon in Residence, his lecture was scheduled for 9.00 a.m. in one of the rooms on Palace Green. He arrived wearing a cassock and carrying his surplice, hood and scarf over an arm. He was well into his subject as the bells started ringing at 9.45 a.m. for Morning Prayer (which was then held at 10.00 a.m.), and he was still in full flow when the 9.55 a.m. five-minute bell began. After further two or three minutes he suddenly seemed to be aware of the bell and said he must finish. He then picked up has papers and robes and left the room just as the 9.59 a.m. bell started—do you still call it 'the agony bell'? *[It's the 'Panic Bell'—Editor]* He sprinted across the grass to the great north door of the cathedral (at the same time trying to put his surplice over his head), and joined the procession of choir and clergy as they emerged from door opposite the one he came in and turned down the central aisle. *(Canon John Gunstone)*

Bishop Michael was guest of honour at the Chad's Day lunch which took place after it had been announced that he was to become the next Archbishop of York. Chad's Day fell in Lent that year and, as was the custom then, the Principal had written to him as Diocesan Bishop formally asking for a dispensation from Lenten observance for the day. Said MR in the course of his speech, "Ever since I came to Durham as your Bishop it has been dispensations for this and for that. But all this must now cease. You can expect something stiffer from the Primate of England!" *(Frank Cranmer, a story picked up when he was writing the history of St Chad's College)*

On a sunny afternoon in May 1974 I was standing next to Michael Ramsey, watching him sign a visitors' book Bishop Michael Cantuar and then write in capital letters CHRIST IS RISEN. We were on a British Council of Churches visit to the German Democratic Republic and were at the heart of Germany, *'Land der Dichter und Denker'*, and in the heartland of the Reformation. But we had left the city of the plain and come up an escarpment into the beech forest or Buchenwald, which had given the place a name of omen. We passed through the gates of the concentration camp and experienced a sudden chill, such as I have felt elsewhere only at Babi Yar, the ravine near Kiev where the Ukrainian Jews were slaughtered. Sometimes evil is tangible. We had come in a short space of time from paradise to paradise lost. There was not much to see, but that only gave more scope to the historical imagination. However, we had to concentrate on the present, for this was potentially the most sensitive moment in the Archbishop's visit to the German Democratic Republic, accompanied as we were by representatives of both church and state and of the state-controlled media. Every word, every gesture, every syllable counted as contemporary Pharisees and Sadducees put questions to the holy man, seeking to entrap him in his answers.

We went into the cell of Paul Schneider, the Lutheran pastor who had sung hymns and preached sermons for his fellow prisoners; and we were shown the whipping block where he had been beaten to death before them for his pains. A word was expected from the Archbishop within a culture which was now threefold a culture of the word—German, Protestant, Marxist-Leninist—where every occasion called forth weighty utterances, sacred and secular. The Archbishop held one of his typical silences and then he prayed, commending the souls of martyred Jews, Christians and socialists alike to the eternal mercy of God, yearning for an end to hatred in the Kingdom of peace and love. This was the second of three occasions during a fraught itinerary on which the Archbishop turned what needed to be said away from immediate concerns into prayer to our Father in heaven. Bishop Schönherr of East Berlin and Brandenburg, the *primus inter pares* of the East German bishops, was later to call it 'the visit of the three prayers'.

Earlier, in Berlin, we had returned to our hotel late on the first evening to be met by a minor disaster. The antiquated plumbing had given out in the archiepiscopal bathroom, which was so dramatically flooded that the water had had to be turned off at the mains. The staff, who had so desperately wanted everything to go right, were distracted in a flurry of inefficiency and obsequiousness. The Archbishop was not at all put out. He sat down with the rest of us on comfortable sofas in the foyer and suggested that we all have 'a nice cup of tea.' To the accompaniment of mysterious noises off we waited, and waited. Eventually an embarrassed manager appeared with a bottle of the best wine and a tray of glasses. "There was," he said, "no water. Would wine do instead?" The Archbishop's eyebrows went up and down; his shoulders heaved; "Yes", he said, "yes. It's happened before, it's happened before. At Cana in Galilee, Cana in Galilee," thus defusing a potentially dangerous moment with mirth and merriment and knowledge of the scriptures.

We visited the Stephanusstift, one of those large diaconal institutions, which German Protestantism had pioneered and which the socialist state was only too glad to allow to continue. Here the non-useful members of society, the educationally sub-normal, the blind and the aged were being cared for at a lower material level certainly than in the West but with love and humanity by deacons and deaconesses whose annual conference was taking place that afternoon. The Archbishop was asked to 'say a word.' He gave a memorable and impromptu exposition of what it means to serve Him whose service is perfect freedom. For a moment the all-pervading greyness of socialist everyday life, the pain of Christian disunity, the horror of so much human suffering heaped up in one place—all this melted away and, as at the preaching of Stephen, we could see the heavens opened and the Son of Man standing at the right hand of God. It is strange that it should have been given to Michael Ramsey, who at times could be so gauche and tongue-tied, to produce these astonishing disclosures, almost theophanies.

This was not the only time it happened on that visit. Indeed it was to occur again in the unlikely setting of a formal dinner at the residence of the British Ambassador, who hosted the Archbishop's party and senior guests from Church and State. The evening game, for such it turned out to be, was played strictly according to British rules, even though it was an away match for us. The East Germans were well-schooled in Soviet etiquette. They had brought long speeches with them in their pockets and were prepared for frequent toasts to peace and friendship. There was no opportunity for any of these things. Instead, the port circulated and more concentrated and focussed conversation ensued. Here the Archbishop was in his element. The ready wit and mellifluous rhetoric, which had characterised the young president of the Cambridge Union came to the fore. If, in theology and spirituality, he sometimes gave the impression of being rather conservative, in politics and public affairs he was a liberal through and through. With the utmost courtesy but with persistence he pressed the statesmen on civil and human rights. They sought refuge in flattery and half-remembered quotations from the laborious speeches languishing in their back pockets. One remarked what an honour it was for them that the Archbishop should visit the German Democratic Republic. "Yes, yes," he replied, "I am an old man and wherever I go, people say nice things to me. But they don't do what I tell them. For example in South Africa." Only Michael Ramsey could have drawn that comparison and, as it were, hit the target by implication and with a calculated *faux pas*.

We visited Eisenach where Bach was born, Pachelbel had been organist and Luther had been a choir boy. Above all it was the place to which Martin Luther, kidnapped on his way home from his lonely stand against Church and Diet of Worms, [*The Diet of Worms 1521 is most memorable for the Edict of Worms (Wormser Edikt), which addressed Martin Luther and the effects of the Protestant Reformation. It was conducted from 28 January to 25 May 1521, with Emperor Charles V presiding — Editor*] was taken and where he made the first translation of the Bible into German from Hebrew and Greek. We went into his room and stood by his desk. What could we say? The Archbishop lifted up his voice and prayed: "Blessed Lord, who hast caused all holy scriptures to be written for our learning; grant that we may in such wise hear them, read, mark, learn and inwardly digest them that by patience and comfort of thy holy word we may embrace and ever hold fast the blessed hope of everlasting life which thou hast given us in our Saviour Jesus Christ." That was the third prayer, not extempore prayer this time but common prayer.

As Archbishop Ramsey advanced towards the Catholic Cathedral, the Bishop came forward to greet him with a speech in sonorous Latin and to lead him into the service, notable for the size and enthusiasm of the congregation. There was a wholeness about this occasion which had been lacking until then. At the end spontaneous applause broke out in the Cathedral and it spread into the streets and squares of the city, contrasting strongly with the usual sullen enforced crowd participation in visits by dignitaries from other communist states. Next day over one hundred Protestant and Catholic students gave the Archbishop a rapturous reception and listened spellbound to his exposition of the state of play and future prospects of the ecumenical movement.

Back in Berlin we met the Head of State, who, in 1961, had been formally responsible for the building of the Berlin Wall. In him, Michael Ramsey was face to face with the incarnation of Stalinist socialism as actually practised in the 1960s and 1970s. Herr Stoph had much to say, the Archbishop little; but he continued to press his questions about cultural exchange and the need for people to meet. Herr Stoph said expected things about the need to bring to an end the Cold War. "Yes", said the Archbishop in one of his sudden unexpected moments of inspiration and in a memorable phrase, "Yes. But there is no point in replacing a cold war with a cold peace. We need a warm peace, in which people meet each other and get to know each other." He paused, and then something remarkable happened. The oblique and fleeting reference to freedom of movement must have touched a chord and a neuralgic point of conscience. Herr Stoph started speaking unscripted about the building of the Wall and the reasons, which had made it necessary. He spoke and spoke; he couldn't stop speaking. The Archbishop sat opposite him, silent, immobile, with his white hair like the snow on a dormant volcano. Still the President went on, for 20 or maybe 30 minutes. His aides and associates were showing visible signs of embarrassment. Eventually he stopped. Everyone was expecting some diplomatic, emollient, even pastoral word from the Archbishop. But he said nothing. This was not just a negative silence, an absence of words. It was a positive silence, an actual act or deed, like the silence of Christ before Pilate. He was doing something which the world could not understand but which those of us who were priests and pastors could. He had just been hearing a confession; but that confession had consisted entirely of self-justification. And because there was no contrition, no sorrow for sin, no intention of amendment of life, the Archbishop was doing one of the most difficult things a priest ever has to do, namely withholding absolution. It was an extraordinary moment in which time stood still. It was like being with Ambrose and Theodosius, or at any one of those turning points in history when spiritual power has confronted worldly power across a table, face to face. In the land of the Berlin Wall and of justification by faith, justification by self had had its say. But the prophet Daniel had already interpreted the writing on the wall: '*Mene, mene, tekel and parsin* — weighed in the balances and found wanting. *Gewogen und zu leicht befunden.* God has numbered the days of your kingdom and brought it to an end.' (Daniel 5:25-28)

Somehow the silence was broken, the atmosphere changed and we returned to the level of discussion and of diplomacy. But no one who was present during that eloquent silence will ever forget it, echoing as it did the cry of Moses before Pharaoh, "Let my people go."

Soon it was our turn to cross over into West Berlin—so easy for us with our British passports and visas, so nearly impossible for 17 million citizens of the German Democratic Republic. As an exceptional concession the drivers were allowed to take us through Checkpoint Charlie to the West Berlin Church Headquarters. They were excited about the prospect of breaking a taboo, confident that they knew the way. Alas, they drove straight into the unlit and uncharted no man's land, which had once been the heart of a great metropolis. Walter Pabst, the senior church functionary who was accompanying us, got out and asked a nearby pedestrian, *"Sprechen Sie deutsch?"*—"Do you speak German?" We wept. After all the highs and lows, the sublime moments and the frustrations of those unforgettable days, it was this little tragi-comic, Chaplinesque, pathetic moment of farce, which disclosed the enormity, the hubris, the wickedness of enforced separation. No wonder that the Epistle to the Ephesians, so beloved by Michael Ramsey and the cornerstone of his ecclesiology, describes our salvation in terms of the breaking down of a wall of separation (Eph 2:14).

When he was in America once he was being harassed by journalists. One of them addressed him as, "Archie" to which he replied "The name's Mick." *[His childhood nickname—Editor.]* On another occasion he was being rather impertinently questioned as to how long he prayed for each day. He thought for a moment and then said "About a minute, yes, yes, about a minute, but it takes me half an hour to get there."

Michael had an autumnal ministry in Durham. People remember seeing him wandering around in his cassock, like a kind of purple cloud and being just as spiritual and eccentric as ever. He loved talking to students and people remember him sitting down in the middle of the road in the Bailey to talk about the Trinity.

Visitors to the Cathedral would come up to him and ask him who he was and he always used to say in his recognisable intonation, "I used to be Bishop of Durham, yes, yes, I used to be Bishop of Durham." Anyone else would have said, "I used to be Archbishop of Canterbury or Archbishop of York" but in his self-understanding what he was was Bishop, and he was Bishop of Durham. To be Archbishop of York or Canterbury was a job he had done temporarily whereas to be Bishop was his identity.

There was a wonderful occasion in Peter Baelz's time when the Cathedral celebrated the 100th anniversary of the founding of Marks and Spencer, and Marks and Spencer paid for the 'Daily Bread' window by Mark Angus. When the time came for the window to be dedicated the Cathedral thought it must do its best and who should be invited to say a few words except Michael Ramsey? The Cathedral was quite splendid and full of anyone who was anyone from the city, the University, the Diocese and the top brass of Marks and Spencer. When the time came, Michael began, "A hundred years ago, yes, yes, a hundred years ago, Mr Marks came from Lithuania, he came from Lithuania, and here he met, here he met, he met … his future colleague." He was the only man in the world who could forget that 'Spencer' goes with 'Marks'! It was a wonderful occasion.

One little personal example: Michael Ramsey once turned me down for a job, a rather junior job in Lambeth Palace. My informant tells me he did this on the ground that, "John Arnold is too interesting, yes, yes, John Arnold is too interesting. What we need is someone more humdrum, someone more humdrum." Then, in a way typical of Michael, he loved coining phrases and then would wander round chanting to himself, on this occasion particularly enjoying saying to himself, "someone more humdrum." I won't tell you what the job was because in fact they got someone more humdrum who was very good at it.

One final story relates to an event at which I was present, when General Synod said goodbye to him. I was at that time an officer of the Synod, Secretary of the Board for Unity, and therefore privileged to be present on the day. Michael Ramsey was presented with most up to date Greek Lexicon. It might have been the up to date edition of Liddell and Scott, or Geoffrey Lampe's 'Patristic Lexicon'. Anyway, it was very handsome and bound in leather. The Secretary General handed it over to him, he opened it and was immediately lost in it because his interest was caught by what he read. The ceremony went on and eventually he came back to reality and everything continued with great good humour. Afterwards the Secretary

General mentioned how gratifying it was that he was enjoying his book and he said, "Yes, yes, yes. I opened it at the word, *phallos!* Very interesting, Very interesting!" He was caught red-handed. *(The Very Revd John Arnold)*

I first encountered Ramsey in 1949 when I came up to Durham as a fresher. He was then Van Mildert Professor of Divinity, but was soon to move to Cambridge as Regius Professor. He was already a man of stature in all senses, tall with high shoulders a big head with deep set eyes and overshadowing eyebrows. He looked a lot older than his years, about mid-40s. A familiar figure to be seen on Palace Green, hurrying to 10 o'clock Matins in the Cathedral after a lecture. Although he was shy in company, he was clearly held in great regard and affection in Durham. He was missed when he went to Cambridge, and there was much rejoicing when he returned to Durham as Bishop in 1952.

Soon after, I decided that this was the bishop I wanted to ordain me, and in whose Diocese I would serve. This was to be fulfilled in 1955. When he first arrived as Bishop there was a great deal of work to do before he could move into Auckland Castle, so he lived in college at St Chad's (where I was then studying for ordination). He was clearly very much at home in the college and at High Table. We undergraduates felt it was a great privilege to have him with us.

In his time, a SPCK [*Society for Promoting Christian Knowlege—Editor*] bookshop was opened in the College. Ramsey opened it and blessed it. In his words of introduction he said: "There is only one sort of person worse than someone who can't talk about theology, and that's someone who can't talk about anything else!" On Sunday afternoons the Ramseys entertained students to tea at their home in the College. We sat at the long dining table, Ramsey at one end, Mrs Ramsey at the other presiding over a large brown enamel teapot. Mrs Ramsey was proactive in finding digs or rooms for students. We were offered a newly converted basement in the house next door under Professor H. E. W. Turner, Lightfoot Professor of Divinity.

Ramsey enjoyed giving talks and lectures. He was a clear communicator, which all could enjoy in 'The Bishoprick' (Diocesan monthly) and later in his 'Durham Essays and Addresses' on a wide range of topics. I have enjoyed and derived much benefit from re-reading his works in recent years, his 'Gospel and Catholic Church' was re-published last year. When he listened to a questioner (e.g. after a talk) he would attend to their spiel, often long and more of a statement of their views. He would indicate he was following their argument by saying, "Yes.............yes..........yes." while they spoke, which could be off-putting to say the least. Then, with twinkle of the deep-set eyes, he would reply, the eyebrows going up and down as did the modulation of his voice. Good entertainment, as his words often were a dig at the self-assurance of his interlocutor!

I felt very proud to serve under him in the Diocese. It was rather sad when he moved to York, but that was to the Church's advantage. I was present at his enthronement at Durham and as Archbishop of York—both unforgettable for his presence, his words and the promise of what was to come. I shall never forget the words of his text at his enthronement at Canterbury from 1 Samuel: 'There went with Saul a band of men whose hearts God had touched.' His heart was certainly touched by God, and he touched the hearts of many others. *(The Revd Canon Humphrey York)*

I was at St Chad's College from 1981-84, when Michael Ramsey was a regular visitor to the chapel, and the college. Shuffling into lunch (a self-service affair) with his characteristic gait, and absent-minded air, he would regularly take his cutlery from the dirty slop bucket, and a quick witted student would have to surreptitiously replace them with clean ones before he tucked in. He supported many college events, but, having little or no small talk, he would often stand quite alone at the drinks afterwards, humming away to himself quite contentedly, until some keen ordinand would spy him alone and beetle up for a conversation on some weighty theological topic. He was a generous host, and I counted myself fortunate to be part of a group of Chadsmen who would go round there on a Tuesday evening for a glass of white burgundy, to hear him speak on perhaps 'the significance of the Eucharist,' or 'ARCIC.' *[Anglican-Roman Catholic International Commission—Editor]*

The latter was particularly memorable, as he summed up the history of relations between Canterbury and Rome from 1500 to 1960 in a most elegant fashion, pausing only to stutter over some particular high (or low!) point. But when he came to his own tenure of that office he would slip from third person to first—"and when the then Archbishop of Canterbury went to Rome, the Pope sat there, and I sat here"!! and he would gaze up with a rheumy eye at the splendid photograph of them both that sat on the mantlepiece. I was at Repton (long after him of course), but it meant he had a soft spot for me, and on graduation day, having done well in my exams, he sought me out through the throng of students and parents and gave me card in which he had written 'Congratulations—*Floreat Repandunum!*' I still have it. He and Mrs Ramsey were just the sweetest Christian couple. *(Richard Hallam)*

As Principal of Lincoln Theological College, AMR interviewed the potential ordinands. One young man was to be interviewed after Evensong and duly presented himself. AMR was given to Quaker-like silences and this young man encountered one. Not a word was spoken for some considerable time (perhaps ten minutes?) when AMR suggested to the applicant, "Mr Smith you may find, yes, you may find Lincoln is a very quiet place!"

During a Durham Pilgrimage to the Abbey of Bec in Normandy one of the brethren related an incident when AMR made a similar pilgrimage as Archbishop of Canterbury. As the procession moved into the Chapter House after the service they were concerned that they didn't have the Archbishop with them. Despatched to find him, the young monk found the Archbishop at the tomb of the Founder in the centre of the nave, with his foot firmly lodged in the grille over the tomb! AMR had a very personalised, irregular gait which on this occasion allowed him to put a foot wrong! (see television footage of the 1953 Coronation procession leaving the Abbey).

During World War Two AMR was appointed Air Raid Warden for the college under the City Air Raid Warden, Mr George Greenwell. Mr Greenwell reported that in an emergency the only way to contact the then

Canon Ramsey was by throwing gravel at his window. Mrs Phyllis Richardson, a college resident at the time, told of the time when AMR, fulfilling his duties, assembled all the College residents on the green in response to the siren. Only to be gently told, "Michael, that was the all clear".

In his small guide to Auckland Castle, Mr E Alexander describes himself as, "Butler and Friend of five Bishops of Durham 1905-58". Mr Alexander had very clear ideas of what Bishops of Durham required across a wide spectrum of activities, including what standards and type of food should be served. Sausage and mash was not amongst the acceptable dishes but it was a particular favourite of AMR. A ruse was devised, AMR said to his wife, "Do you know what we had for lunch today in the House of Lords?" "No dear" replied Mrs Ramsey—"Delicious sausage and mash" all this in the hearing of Mr Alexander. Within the week sausage and mash appeared on the menu! *(Denis Trigg)*

I was in my Final year at Hatfield College in 1979 and Michael Ramsey occasionally came to the college chapel to celebrate Communion as we were between college chaplains. On one occasion I was invited to join him and the chapel clerk at High Table and afterwards in the SCR. He and Lady Ramsey were convivial and at ease, but we had to remember to pass the port round in the right direction!

A little later he stopped me in the Bailey and invited both myself and the chapel clerk (Piers Davey, now an Anglican priest serving in Australia) for sherry and cheese straws towards the end of the afternoon of the landmark May 1979 General Election. Lady Ramsey's cheese straws were very delicious and I ate quite a few of them! Lord Ramsey was disappointed that—as a "peer of the realm" as he put it—he could not vote in the General Election and he very much wanted to place his vote. Neither of us dared to ask for which party he would have voted!

I can't remember much more of our conversations that day but apart from politics, both the Ramseys were interested in what our futures might hold after graduation and what student life was like in Hatfield College. After graduation he and I exchanged letters—mainly in reply to my queries about being a Christian in today's world. He never forgot who I was and said he prayed for everyone he met. His deep Christian faith and spirituality shone through and I am sure he meant it! He had a way of furrowing his brow and saying "yesss" which I found enabled me to feel at ease in his presence. I feel privileged to have known both the Ramseys. *(Stephen Mott)*

I shall never forget 'sitting at his feet' at a retreat in Low Fell, Gateshead, nor his enormous impact during my time at Cambridge. And of course, his phenomenal memory for names! (*Canon Tony Meakin*)

My mum always equated hospitality with the offer of abundant food. I recall Michael's delight in her chocolate/brandy sauce, one Lent, on his 'visitation' and in conducting us making music from those suck-blow whistle things that were got from musical crackers one Christmas time! To me in my youth he seemed a man entirely without guile, warm hearted, open, human, yet, dare I say it, full of the Holy Spirit. There seemed to be a very direct spirituality with him. *(Mr P. Piper)*

I knew Michael Ramsey during my boyhood in Durham Cathedral Choir. We rarely left The College precincts during the war, and consequently saw a great deal of the Dean and Chapter going about their duties.

I still think of him as Canon Ramsey, as he was then, an eccentric but wonderful man who seemed to know everything except what day it was! On Sunday mornings, two of the senior choristers took the collection along the Quire, as they still do, but in those days we had to include the back row of the Chapter. That was no problem until we came to Canon Ramsey, who never seemed to have any money with him. The organist often had to fill in while he fussed around his person, eventually giving up and waving us on, leaving the *Cantoris* boy with the blame for making everyone late in getting to the Altar. Our theory was that he had probably put some change in his trouser pocket, but had forgotten the trousers under the cassock!

Now and then he took us for some Latin. Whenever he would ask us a question and we replied with the wrong answer, he would raise one of his large busy eyebrows and say, "Hmm?" We soon caught on that this was our signal to change the answer.

Despite his apparent disinterest in various mundane matters, his wit and intellect were incomparable. I remember sitting quite near to him at a Durham Cathedral Old Chorister Asociation dinner while the then Chapter Clerk, Rear Admiral Laybourne, was recounting one of his naval anecdotes as part of his speech. Near the end of the tale he referred to someone as a 'silly bugger'. There was a rather horrified silence as the speaker turned towards Canon Ramsey and apologised. "That's perfectly all right, Mr Laybourne" came the immediate reply, "A term of endearment in the north -east, I've noticed".

During the war the Cathedral was run by virtually a skeleton staff, as most of the able-bodied men were away. Any guiding was done by the Dean or some member of the Chapter immediately after a service, and I think there were about three vergers. Fire-watching duties were also shared amongst the Chapter, and it is slightly disconcerting as I write to think of Canon Ramsey being our first line of protection; a man who probably would not have noticed if his cassock had caught fire!

One of our friends (himself now a knight of the realm) used to keep us in fits of laughter in the dormitory with wonderful impersonations of him. As young boys we thought Ramsey as an eccentric, but above all, we were extremely fond of him. He was always kind to us, especially at Christmas, when he knew that we were away from home. I cannot think of anything more suitable to his memory than a window, as it was through him that many people found light in their lives. It was an honour to have known him. *(George Hetherington)*

My fondest memory is of walking through the cloisters with him after an Empire Youth Sunday Evensong when I had read the First Lesson on behalf of the Scouts. I met my parents in the cloisters and Michael came out of the Chapter House and spoke to my father whom he knew, and whilst walking through to The College talking to my parents he dropped his arm round my shoulders in a perfectly natural gesture. This was some 60 years ago but I don't think the memory of that afternoon will ever fade. *(K. L. Hayton)*

When I was Principal of St John's and living at 7 South Bailey, the Ramseys moved into the White House opposite. I was not sure how he would react to my appointment as the first female Principal of St John's College but he was very supportive. It was quite intimidating to find him standing on my doorstep for the first time when I was the new Principal. But no Archbishop of Canterbury ever held terrors for me again.

The Cranmer students started popping across to talk to him so he heard a lot of the news from their perspectives. A situation arose which required delicate handling by The College and we were taking action behind the scenes but keeping confidentiality. There was to be a big dinner at Cranmer Hall and Ramsey was to be the guest of honour. On the day of the dinner he phoned me up and told me he couldn't come under the circumstances, which he had heard from some of the students who only knew part of the story. I had to reprove the Archbishop and asked him to remember how he handled such situations when he was Archbishop. I reminded him that before he accepted the students' version he should check the facts. He agreed and said, "You are quite right. May I come to the dinner?" I was struck by his humility in admitting that he was wrong in this instance and his readiness to redress it.

He walked down the Bailey oblivious of the traffic and waving to people as he went. Once I asked him, "What do you do with all the people who stop you and ask you to pray for them?" He replied, "I say 'yes', do it immediately, and then forget about it."

There was a sort of innocence about him which included taking a bath in an un-curtained bathroom in full view of my house. My elderly mother was living with me and one evening when the light was on in the bathroom she said to me, "I think I've seen more of the former Archbishop of Canterbury since being here than I ever did of your father!"

He was very generous with his time to the students. He gave a series of lectures in spirituality in the Cranmer lecture room. I remember him speaking once about his reluctance as a young don to go to a parish and how he'd been almost resentful about it. Then, looking straight at the ordinands, he said, "It was probably the most important piece of training I had, to learn to be a curate in an ordinary parish." It was very costly to him.

He was very restless. He lived at the top of South Street to begin with and wasn't too happy there. Then he moved to the Bailey for about three years and then went to York. I sensed he was always looking for something. Joan was splendid, she had a glorious sense of humour and was very good at being gatekeeper to him. She would give hints about the best way into a topic you wanted to discuss with him. His sense of humour was different, he had a very strong sense of irony. *(Dr Ruth Etchells)*

I remember a service at St Nic's at which Michael Ramsey was the invited preacher. On the procession in, that opened the service, Michael was taking up the rear, walking in his usual doddery way. He positively refused any help struggling up the few steps to the platform on which all the clergy etc. were arraying themselves. To see him beaming around the congregation from underneath those huge eyebrows while holding his hymn book upside down during the first hymn was a sight for sore eyes, but, to be honest, he did not seem with it at all—and you feared for the forthcoming sermon. However when it came, the sermon was crystal clear, like a rare diamond, containing enormous meaning with an economy of words. When it was finished he immediately reverted to his doddery behaviour, and how he got off the platform safely to bring up the rear of the outgoing procession, again positively refusing any aid, was a minor miracle. As the clergy procession wound its way out he passed in front of his wife in the front row and gave an enormous wink—and you were left wondering if, perhaps, throughout, you had been fortunate enough to witness an intended element of theatre. *(Prof Alan Martin)*

When I was a curate in Darlington, Michael Ramsey visited the church and stayed for lunch afterwards. Knowing that he could be taciturn, my training incumbent had told me that I had to make sure the conversation flowed during the meal and he would kick me under the table if I needed to make more effort. During the meal he told Michael Ramsey of this arrangement and Ramsey said, "Kicking someone under the table requires a faculty."

After the memorial service for Michael Ramsey, Joan was near the font at the back of the Cathedral greeting people as they left. She knew nearly everyone's name, she was awfully good at that. *(Canon Patrick Kent)*

It was after I had been appointed Cathedral Architect at Durham (1976-98) that I came to know Mrs Phyllis Richardson and Lord and Lady Ramsey after they had retired and lived in Durham, attending Cathedral services regularly. At a luncheon arranged by Mrs Richardson in her home in South Street, the Ramseys and I were fellow guests. I remember the conversation turning to 'which person in history each of us would have liked to be'. I should have liked to have been the 'First Master' who first designed the Cathedral, and then to have known the answers to all my questions about the original design. I have racked my memory on what Michael or Joan Ramsey had replied, but without avail. It is one of those questions that will never be answered.

Another recollection about Michael Ramsey arose from his short time as Archbishop of York. I had joined George Charlewood FRIBA in 1958, when he was extending Aklam Church in Middlesbrough, and though I was not involved I was taken to see it by Mr Charlewood as it neared completion. Although I did not attend the consecration by the Archbishop of York, I remember hearing from George Charlewood that during the sermon the somewhat rotund Archbishop had become stuck in the rather narrow pulpit. *(Ian Curry)*

I was at St Chad's College (Anglo-Catholic in its churchmanship) one Ash Wednesday when Michael Ramsey called in and was talking to a group of students. Another student came in from an Ash Wednesday service at St Nic's (a low evangelical church) and told us where he had been. Michael Ramsey looked at him and said, "No, no. Surely you can't have been there" to which the student replied that he had. Michael Ramsey then shook his head and said, "Silly boy; silly, silly boy." *(A member of the clergy)*

When Michael Ramsey had retired he visited parishes in the diocese to confirm people. He was always careful to ask, "Does the Bishop of Durham approve?" even though it had already been arranged with the Bishop's office. *(A member of the Cathedral community)*

My earliest memory of Michael Ramsey is of his enthronement in Durham Cathedral. A friend and I, both in our first undergraduate term in Durham (autumn 1952), decided that we would like to go to this service. It was the first I attended in the Cathedral. Sadly, my memories are vague. I do remember that we were taken to seats at the back of the south transept so our involvement was somewhat limited. I remember the three knocks on the door and the solemn procession down the nave. What occurred in the quire is really unknown. I remember being impressed by all the legal jargon that accompanied the enthronement and began to understand the meaning of Established Church.

Bishop Ramsey (as he then was) could often be seen in Durham. I recall one sighting in particular when I passed him on Palace Green during a heavy downpour. He was huddled in raincoat and hat (as was I) but he did look up and smile, warmly, at my "good afternoon". Our own 'fellow feeling' for him was in his Morris Minor (of which we saw pictures). One was our first car at that time! My memory of him in Durham is very happy. *(John Pottinger)*

Michael Ramsey and his wife gave a home to German Jewish refugee children. I was a pupil at the girls' grammar school in Durham and in about 1943 there were two German Jewish girls in the school. One was a

10, Downing Street,
Whitehall.—

Confidential.   17th June, 1952.

Dear Mr. Dean,

     I am writing to inform you
that The Queen has approved the
nomination of Canon A.M. Ramsey to
the Bishopric of Durham. The
announcement will be made in the
morning newspapers of Wednesday,
the 18th June.

     I thought that you would like
to know of this in advance, but it
is of course confidential until the
morning of the 18th.

     Yours sincerely,

                   (signature)

   The Very Reverend
     The Dean of Durham.

P.S. This is a duplicate of a letter
     sent yesterday to Durham.

BY HAND.
Confidential.

     The Very Reverend
       The Dean of Durham,

        Church Assembly,

         Church House,

           Dean's Yard,

           Westminster. S.W. 1.

A letter from the Prime Minister's Office announcing the appointment of
Michael Ramsey as Bishop of Durham (from the Durham Cathedral Archives)

DURHAM CATHEDRAL

ORDER OF SERVICE

AT THE

ENTHRONEMENT

OF THE

RIGHT REVEREND

ARTHUR MICHAEL RAMSEY

AS BISHOP OF THE DIOCESE

ON

The Feast of St. Luke the Evangelist

SATURDAY, 18th OCTOBER, 1952

at 3 p.m.

The front cover of the Order of Service for the Enthronement of Michael Ramsey as Bishop of Durham (from the Durham Cathedral Archives) particular friend of mine and I visited her at Canon Ramsey's house in The College. I do not know how many children were helped by the Ramseys or for how long. *(Audrey Kelly)*

My husband and his family lived in Church Lane in poor quality housing—parents and four children in two rooms. When the Archbishop went to the house he was appalled at the conditions in which they lived and shortly afterwards the family was re-housed in a three bedroomed house in Alington Place which was owned by the Church Army.

I attended Durham Girls' Grammar School. In either 1953 or 1954 the Archbishop presented me with a prize at speech day. He told a lovely tale about Winston Churchill at Westminster Abbey on Coronation day. He said Sir Winston was like an excited schoolboy and would not take his place in the Abbey until he had seen the Queen arrive.

Our joint memories are of seeing the Archbishop walking through Durham when he came back here to live when he retired. He was a familiar figure in the city and spoke to everyone he passed. *(Milly and Eric Robinson)*

One freezing winter's day, snow and ice on the ground, I was walking up what that day was virtually sheet ice, trying to keep my balance, from Prebends Bridge towards the Water Gate and the Bailey, when Michael appeared through the arch heading gingerly in the opposite direction, for his 'constitutional', but not at all sure of his footing. Accordingly, he lost it and ended up in a heap at my feet, muttering, "Oh dear, Oh dear" (or similar!). There was no-one else around and I helped him up back onto his feet again—he was a big man—brushed him down etc. After he'd pulled himself together, and we'd checked he could still move his limbs and was fit to carry on as intended, he commented, "Rather slippery today," and was only concerned that I was alright! Lovely man. *(Richard Hird)*

In those days the gatehouse post box by the arch was emptied at 4.00 p.m. At 3.45 p.m. each day Ramsey, clutching a collection of envelopes, would walk to the post box. One afternoon I found myself walking with him. "Are you busy these days?" I ventured. "O yes" he said. "I'm preparing for my death."

In 1975 Ramsey delivered the annual Pastoral Theology Lectures in Durham. His subject was 'Holy Spirit'. Not 'the' Holy Spirit he explained at great length, but Holy Spirit.

He and Lady Ramsey sometimes came into Cranmer for their evening meal. There was no 'high table' atmosphere. They were rather unceremonial occasions. He was approachable and friendly to students and staff seemingly at home with plain food and basic facilities. *(The Revd Rosemary Nixon)*

I was Precentor at the Cathedral from 1980 to 1984 and Bishop Ramsey took turns in the daily celebrations rota which I organised. Soon after our daughter was born I received a letter which read, "My dear Nigel, Our congratulations on the lovely family news. We are both so happy to know of your great happiness and send you all our love, Bishop Michael Ramsey." I was amazed that a childless former archbishop should take the trouble to write so generously to a young priest, and the note remains a treasured possession.

Something of the same transcendence of his own situation was evident in his Cathedral sermon on the centenary of the Royal College of Midwives. His text was John 16.21, and I do not think that any hearer who did not know would have imagined that he himself never saw the birth of a child. *(The Revd Nigel Warner)*

My main Durham recollection of Bishop Michael has become a family legend. Our daughter Katie, now a 30 year old Mum, was a toddler in a pushchair and on a day when we were walking up the Bailey he was on his way home to the White House, opposite St John's College. He was wearing his purple cassock. We were fast gaining on him when Katie's eyes fastened on him and she said (at toddler volume), "Mummy, that man is a lady." As we passed him, her head swivelled to get a better view, and she was satisfied. "Mummy, he *is* a lady, he's wearing a dress". Bishop Michael heard it all. The eyes twinkled, and the eyebrows moved rapidly up and down, but of course he said nothing. (*The Revd David Grieve*)

I recall a study day on John's Gospel at which Michael Ramsey, well into retirement, fielded questions. The setting was the Deanery Solarium. Someone asked quite simply, "What are we to understand by John's expression 'the Word' in relation to Jesus?" Bishop Michael gave a very considerable answer but it is the profound simplicity of his opening which I remember verbatim. He said, "When we speak of Jesus as 'the Word of God' we mean that Jesus is what God has to say about himself." Somehow for me this short sentence summed up and still sums up the wonderful combination of gifts which was Michael Ramsay: sincerity of devotion, depth of insight, clarity of expression. (*The Revd Tom Jamieson*)

Last year, I do not know why, my thoughts turned to Michael Ramsey. I was sadly lacking in knowledge of him, but increasingly aware in my mind's eye of a venerable-like man, strong features, prominent eye brows, a twinkle in the eye and welcoming smile, yet I knew very little of his ministry.

I decided to look for information. I called at Southwell Minster and there in the bookshop I made enquiries. Following a series of unusual incidents I came away with the book 'Through the Year with Michael Ramsey'. One of the staff told me that her family had met Michael Ramsey—he was their son's mentor at Durham.

Now with great thankfulness, in retirement, I look back on the many blessings of my life. Truly, each day with Michael Ramsey brings devotional thoughts and practice, and I quote from a Southwell Minster prayer, 'May I glimpse the glory of God and know His love revealed in Jesus Christ our Lord.' Amen. (*Hilda I Mulley*)

In his retirement Bishop Michael would preach from time to time in the college chapel at St Chad's where I was an undergraduate (1982-85). I vividly remember that he would preach wonderful sermons from half a dozen words written on the back of an envelope—one of the earliest recyclers and a measure of the man's mind.

He would hold seminars in his home in the Bailey to which would be invited undergraduates of all faiths and none. These meetings would tackle some of the burning issues of the day in a stimulating and accessible way. Even in old age and physically frail he could hold the attention of this group of young people for a good hour and half and always left them wanting more—although the wine may have helped things along too!

I also have memories of 'Eucharistic mishaps'—consecrated wafers would flutter to the floor in the early morning sunlight—like Manna in the wilderness—but because it was Bishop Michael it never seemed to matter and never detracted from the celebration.

I once spent a long vacation working with the craftsmen on the Cathedral. After a few weeks' experience and under gentle supervision I was allowed to lay some reclaimed bricks to form a simple pattern either side of some newly-laid stone steps which led into a Cathedral exhibition space under the Prior's Hall. I think they are still there but Michael would fuel my pride in referring to them often as 'Wayne's steps'.

For me he was one of the great eccentrics so sadly missed in the Church of England of today. In these days where image is all I know of no-one less image conscious but with more true appeal than Michael and I feel honoured to have known him and to have sat at his feet. *(Revd Wayne Plimmer)*

I have a vivid recollection of meeting him on a train travelling up to Durham. When we both got out at Durham, I recall the ticket inspector greeting him with the word, "Welcome back, Bishop." Also I think on one occasion a train which was going south and not stopping in Durham, was halted at Durham simply to pick Bishop Michael up. Of course he was a regular (and very intimidating) presence in the Cathedral. This was during my chairing of the Anglo-Lutheran International Commission, a consequence of which was my frequent quotations from Luther and Lutheran resources. On one occasion he preached magnificently in the Cathedral on the invocation of the saints, and when I thanked him for his sermon he said at once, "Yes, and not a word of Lutheran theology!"

As Van Mildert Professor, I used to hold monthly theological discussions in my study in No 14 The College. Quite by accident on one occasion, AMR spied a copy of his book, 'The Gospel of the Catholic Church' open on my desk (which was one of the books I used to teach ecclesiology) he said at once, "What are you doing with that old fashioned theology?" He had, of course, moved considerably from the Barthian emphasis of that work. *(The Rt Revd Stephen Sykes)*

I remember serving as an altar boy for him, during a service at St John's Church, Meadowfield, where my father was organist. It was, if memory serves, late 1953, not long after the Coronation, and having watched on the Queen's right at the service in Westminster Abbey (on TV of course) and also having seen the feature films 'Elizabeth is Queen' and 'A Queen is Crowned' at the Essoldo and Palladium cinemas in the city, I felt very important, being in such close proximity to him.

My childish impression was of a very large man with a kindly face. Many years later, after his retirement, I can recall seeing him often, walking around the city, invariably smiling and greeting people, people he wouldn't know, but still taking the trouble to pass the time of day with them.

Perhaps the fact that I can recall, after all these years such clear memories of him says all we need to know about him. *(Alan Hillery)*

On one occasion after his retirement he was invited to give a pastoral theology lecture, at St Chad's. As he was the speaker, a number of non-theologians, including me attended. After the lecture there were questions, and a rather showing-off postgraduate student asked, in more or less the following words: "But surely, Archbishop, Wittgenstein said …" With a sweet smile and the utmost courtesy, Michael Ramsey replied: "I really don't think that the man in the pew is particularly interested in Wittgenstein."

I regret that I can't be more precise about the date and the occasion, but it was definitely a pastoral theology lecture, and I do perfectly remember Michael Ramsey's words, putting the brash young man in his place without humiliating him. *(Dr Anne Orde)*

My main memories when I taught at Durham School (1979-82) are of attending the midweek early morning Eucharist in the Cathedral at which he and Joan were very regular attendees (which was something that could not be said of any members of the Chapter at the time!!) He was always recollected and prayerful, would always say hello, and over the three years I was there his prayerful presence had a considerable impact on me. When I was ordained a deacon my brother-in-law was Chaplain of Chad's and I had my post-ordination party in his house on Old Bailey and Bishop Michael and Joan attended it briefly which was a great honour. I have two lovely letters he wrote to me on the occasion of my ordination as a deacon and as a priest which I treasure. *(The Revd Canon Mark Bonney)*

Michael, on giving godly counsel once at the end of confession: "Go home, put your feet up and have a gin and tonic with the Lord." *(The Venerable Peter Townley)*

During the three years I spent training for ordained ministry at Cranmer Hall (1985-88), Michael Ramsey used to come to lecture on John's Gospel to the whole college. I have a vivid memory of him being escorted across the road from his house to the Cranmer lecture hall where he would speak movingly about the themes in the discourses in chapters 14-17, bringing them to life in ways that connected them with national life in the 80s. He was, by this time, losing his sight but I recall the way in which he could recite great chunks of the text from memory, breaking off to put a gloss here, a word of explanation there, and returning to the text without faltering. He was a man steeped in scripture, prayer and social concern and was a great inspiration to us all.

I also recall travelling up to Durham on an East Coast mainline train for an interview at Cranmer Hall (this must have been in the autumn or winter of 1985). There were strikes in the National Health Service at the time. I was working as a nurse at Addenbrooke's hospital in Cambridge and fell into conversation with another nurse from Peterborough who happened to be sitting opposite me. Neither of us was particularly aware of the man in the corner, behind a newspaper, until Michael Ramsey looked out (recognizable by his wonderful eyebrows!) and said, "This is most interesting, ladies." He spent the rest of the journey up to Durham quizzing us about our views on the Health Service, the sustainability of a 'free at the point of delivery' principle, and the moral question of whether those in the caring professions should ever withdraw their labour for what might be perceived as the 'greater good' of persuading a government to put more resources into health care. What struck me was his humility in listening to the stories and opinions of a couple of very junior nurses who probably thought they could see the solution to problems they scarcely understood. He seemed really interested in the small details of our work. *(The Venerable Janet Henderson)*

Michael Ramsey was young when he came to Durham, but already looked old enough to be a canon. During his first winter he was due to preach, and Dean Alington told his house party to take a good look at the preacher, because one would never have thought he was only 35. But on the Saturday evening, he sent a note to my father (then Archdeacon of Durham), saying that he had got quinsy, and would not be able to deliver his sermon. He had, however written it out, and please could my father deliver it for him. My father did, and the Dean's guests found it impossible to believe that he, actually in his 60s, was only 35.

Michael's house, next to ours, was much too big for him, then a bachelor, and he made the top floor available to us, and I think to John Owen, the son of the Bishop of Jarrow, as play rooms, in which I was able to lay out all my

Hornby gauge 0 track. I think we may have misbehaved. I have a faint memory of his once coming up and being cross with us and the arrangement was not continued.

In the winter of 1941-42 John Owen was at Winchester facing School Certificate. I was due to try for a scholarship. Michael gave us several lessons to try and improve our Greek. I remember in particular learning to conjugate *timao tau iota mu alpha omega*. The imperative could be mispronounced 'tomato'. John found this excruciatingly funny. I have a clear memory of his being doubled up with mirth, while I was sitting on Michael's head. In retrospect I suspect that he was not good at keeping order, and would not have made a good school master. Nevertheless he

12 The College, the Ramsey's house when Michael Ramsey was Canon Professor

put up with us for several sessions, and is one of those to whom I have reason to be very grateful for helping me to win a scholarship.

Michael used to be seen going for walks, his head revolving round an axis only distantly connected to his feet [I can't think of the right word—'staggering', 'swaggering', 'swaying' 'swivelling; 'rollicking'—none is quite right]. We assumed that he was meditating on the Trinity, and his mind was only tenuously connected with the world around him. On one occasion he was conscripted to join in a cricket match at the Archery Club. I have no clear memory of this, being equally averse to games, but it may have been the case that he and I were selected as umpires, as being the place we could do least harm.

Michael sometimes crossed swords with the Dean who had been a Headmaster, and sometimes forgot that canons were not Assistant Masters. The Dean had a penchant for putting in stained-glass windows made by Easton. On one occasion when he was pressing the Chapter to put in yet another one, Michael was heard to intone, *sotto voce,* "Not through eastern windows only, when morning comes in the light.".

Michael married Joan Hamilton, who had been secretary to the Bishop of Jarrow, and been living in The College, when we arrived in 1939. She had seen my father and mother get out of our car, and thought my father resembled Pooh Bear, and named us the Poohs. The name stuck, and Michael knew us as the Poohs. Michael and Joan invented many other nicknames. Canon Jack Richardson was 'Kumkum'; James Duff (the Warden of the Durham Colleges) was 'Willow Herb'; and later in Cambridge, Simon Barrington-Ward (later Bishop of Coventry) was 'Actually Sir''. We went to their wedding in the Galilee Chapel: I think we were forming a voluntary choir. I remember hearing the grown-ups saying that the worst trouble that could befall them was to come back to the house and find that the boiler had gone out.

My father several times told me that he saw in Michael a future Archbishop of Canterbury. Certainly many saw him a Bishop of Durham. Michael was appointed to the Regius Chair of Divinity at Cambridge and as they were preparing to leave Durham for Cambridge, Joan got jaundice (which was what his brother died of). They stayed in our house while she was ill. He did not drive (his mother had been killed in a driving accident). I acted as his driver when he was going to preach at Darlington. After the service, as we were about to go, the Vicar said good-bye, and then added some words which I cannot remember exactly, but were to the effect that he looked forward to seeing Michael back in Durham again, as Bishop. It was a widely shared sentiment. And four years later Alwyn moved from Durham to Winchester, his natural home, and the question of who should succeed him was real. As I remember it (my brother, Paul, has a slightly different memory) the Patronage Secretary came to Durham; Dean Wild said he was new to the diocese, and sent him on to see my father. My father told him that the diocese wanted Michael, and told him of various clergy—Canon Jack Richardson among them—who would bear him out. The Patronage Secretary said that Michael was not wanted by the ecclesiastical powers and so asked if my father could drum up support elsewhere. My father had been an undergraduate friend of Lord Halifax, and agreed to write to him to press Michael's case. It is said that Macmillan said, "Fisher may have been Ramsey's headmaster, but he was not mine".

[Not a Durham tale] At the end of their lives Michael and Joan used sometimes come to us for Sunday lunch at Postmasters' Hall, Merton Street. We had a picture in our hall of our younger son, Richard, with the other members of the Standing Committee of the Cambridge Union. Although his sight was failing, Michael would immediately recognise it as a Cambridge Union picture. Although his Presidency had pointed to a career he did not follow, it was still very much alive in his mind. *(John R. Lucas)*

Perhaps I should explain my first connection with Michael Ramsey. Reggie Cant, who had taught at Durham when Michael was there, was instrumental in suggesting my first curacy where the vicar was a product of St Columba's, Sunderland. While I was still at Cuddesdon, Michael asked me come and see him at Bishopthorpe. He lent me two books to prepare me for Middlesbrough. Then there was lunch, brought to a close by Joan rather evidently kicking him under the table. I was handed over to the chaplain who showed me around. As I left a taxi was coming up the drive which, I was told, was Madame Tussaud. Our ordination on 28th May 1961 was Michael's last in York.

My next encounter with Michael was in 1964 when he came to Durham to open the new St Chad's building (and with another engagement which I can't remember). I was just beginning my second curacy which had turned out to be as domestic chaplain to Bishop Maurice Harland, Michael's successor at Durham. The Ramseys would be staying at Auckland Castle. We were lined up to welcome them. The Bishop said, "I think you know my chaplain". "Yes, yes" said Michael. "I ordained him. I ordained him. And I think it took" (which is a very nice thing for him to remember).

The Ramseys' affection for Auckland was obvious. The castle has three main staircases. Mrs Harland took the Ramseys up the family stairs to the guest room and its adjoining bathroom. I took the archbishop's chaplain up the middle stairs to where he would be sleeping. As I came back to the landing Michael emerged from the other door of the guest bathroom, looked all round the rather grand stairwell, said, "I created that bathroom. I created that little chapel. Yes, that is all I created" and went back into the bathroom.

In my time at the cathedral (1983-92) the arrangement for who celebrates the 7.30 am Eucharist on what day and where was not so amenable as Chadwick describes (p 388). The Precentor prepared a list of future dates, with any variations, and sent it round The College so that, in turn, we could make our choices. It went first to the Dean, then to the Sub-Dean and so on. Bishop Ramsey was at the bottom. This meant that he could land at an awkward altar. The Saturday one, for example, had a patterned carpet which made the exact location of the step difficult for Michael's sight. I never heard him complain.

In those years there was an American summer school in the Castle which usually produced extra worshippers in the Cathedral. On one memorable occasion the Americans heard that the former Archbishop of Canterbury would be the next morning's celebrant. They came in such numbers that the vergers had to rush some seating into the transept for the overflow. Fortunately I had a priest friend staying with me and we were able to help Michael cope with the crowd. Afterwards he said to Joan, "The Cogg was there!" Joan said to Michael, "Did you see those two nice young priests who we met at Nashotah House?"

Walking half-way home with the Ramseys on those early mornings was a delightful experience. They would be arm in arm but his judgement of widths was so variable that sometimes Joan seemed to be scraped against the Deanery garden wall. They enjoyed reporting amusing encounters and seemed to have perfected the art of entertaining each other.

In 1984 the Daily Bread window was welcomed with an event at the west end of the nave. Peter Baelz was sensitive about M & S's Jewish origins so it was not planned to be any form of Christian worship. All sorts of appropriate people were invited including some of M & S's Durham staff. The Dean introduced, the choir sang and Michael spoke. Peter's idea was that Michael was without doubt Durham's most distinguished citizen and it was in that role that we had asked him to speak, not as a bishop etc. Michael did not seem to be bothered with these sensitivities. He gave a breezy account of M & S's origins, meditated on the significance of the archangel Michael as a trademark and generally rejoiced in the firm's generosity and the Cathedral's acquisition.

We, the neighbours, knew that when Joan went down to M & S in the market place with her shopping bag on wheels, with cobbles and pavements and the uphill return, it was not an easy journey. Sometimes she needed help at the check-out. The Ramseys admitted to liking M & S's ready-made sandwiches. I thought of all this when we were trying to find a seat for her at the refreshments after the window event. She ended up at a table of M & S shop assistants.

In Michael's time as Bishop of Durham, St Columba's, Southwick, Sunderland was a great parish for training curates. There were usually three at a time and several of them were glad to overstay the usual initial three or four years. Michael had a soft spot for St Columba's although the area was much changed and the staff reduced. In June 1984 he accepted an invitation to preach at their patronal festival. I had been invited too but, not having a car, was no help with the transport. The Vicar pulled strings and we had door-to-door transport in a luxurious undertaker's limousine. Michael was clearly pleased to be there again, managed the pulpit and preached from what looked like only a few notes in large writing.

The retirement years at Durham saw what must have been the last of the Ramseys' annual holidays in Devon. The Slype in the Cathedral was a kind of behind-the-scenes crossroads for all that is going on and I remember that it was there that I asked them, on their reappearance, how they had enjoyed their holiday. Of course they had: familiar ground and familiar faces. But, on the return journey there was no 'buffit' (Michael's pronunciation) on the train. So when the train stopped at Sheffield he got out, found a buffit on the platform, bought two cups of tea and carried them back onto the train. Joan was enormously proud of him, but my mind was boggling at how he managed it.

When the Ramseys were wondering if they might find someone to replace their housekeeper so that they could continue to live in Durham, Mrs Jenkins, the Bishop's wife was eager to help. She rang me up because she had heard of someone who might be suitable and who lived in part of the diocese which I knew well. I spoke to the Vicar who gave her a good report: apparently she had been in the cosmetics business. A trial visit was arranged. I was away at the time. When I came back, was passing Number 16 and saw the outer door open and thought I would call. Joan emerged from the kitchen and hesitated before opening the glass inner door. "I wondered who it was," she said. "You look so—black." I promised that next time I would wear pink. "Oh, that's not our favourite colour just now," said Joan. And Michael appeared from his study saying, "not pink. No, not pink. Clearly the lady had not passed her test. We went on to talk of other things. *(Revd Tony Hart)*

What I would say about Michael Ramsey (whom I knew over a long period from my schooldays) is that following Cosmo Gordon Lang, William Temple *and* Geoffrey Fisher (the previous Archbishops of Canterbury), Michael Ramsey was a match for each of them and in certain ways he outmatched them because of his depth of spirituality combined with an outstanding grasp of biblical theology. No archbishop in modern times has been able to explain, convey or communicate deep spiritual wisdom and penetrating insight into the meaning of the Christian faith to the extent that he managed, and by so doing enthral and enlighten all who heard him, came into contact with him or who read his published works.

I first knew him when he was the sub-warden of Lincoln Theological College in the 1930s, when he was a young man. He came regularly to the school in Canterbury (St Edmund's) to spend a day or two to preach. My headmaster, Canon Henry Balmforth had been his sixth form Classics Master at Repton School and had a close relationship with him. Michael Ramsey would come into the school library (about 1935-38, he came each year) to browse. At the time he was working on his book 'The Gospel and the Catholic Church' which caused quite a sensation when it came out. We had regular visiting preachers, bishops and other illustrious clergy, but Michael Ramsey even at that stage of his life stood out as having a special gift as a preacher. I remember a sermon he preached probably in 1936 or 1937 on the text 2 Samuel 23:15 (or 2 Chronicles 11:17-18), 'David longed and said, "Oh that one would give me a drink of the water of the well of Bethlehem which is by the gate!' In those days preachers always took a biblical text, and I remember to this day (and I am now 87) the effect his sermon had on me. I had never heard anything like it in power of concentration and impressive delivery. He managed then and later to accentuate the word, "Oh!" "Oh! that one would give me". I used to remind him afterwards of this sermon. Then he struck us as having great gifts and an outstanding spiritual depth and we always looked forward to his visits.

I went to Durham rather than Oxbridge to be one of his first students, as he had become in the 1940s Professor of Divinity. In Durham he was as impressive as ever and his sermons and lectures were avidly awaited, heard and appreciated. He quickly made a mark both in the Cathedral as a preacher and in the University for his gripping and fascinating lectures. He also organised evening meetings and enjoyed with others the expositions and critical comments on the gospels. He was my tutor for at least a year. I used to take my essays to read to him in his large house in The College. It was quite a remarkable and awe-inspiring, an awesome experience to read the essay aloud to him. He maintained total silence even after reading the essay and then usually made one compelling comment which summed up the inadequacy as well as any merit. He was always encouraging even though he was on a different plane.

I realise that many people will still be in Durham who remember Michael Ramsey as Bishop. They will all remember him and will have their own memories of him. But I would just say—as his biographer and others have acknowledged—that nothing that may be said or written about him can possibly convey the person he was and which only his presence and personal knowledge of him could even partially enable him to be seen as he really was.

His presence always gave one the vivid impression of a larger world than the one normally experienced. He seemed to have a grasp of the spiritual dimension, which gave one courage to believe. He was a such a status that his impact as Archbishop on the Church of England can only be compared with the effect that at a later date Cardinal Basil Hume had on the Roman Catholic community. They were both seen as Archbishops of special and unusual and genuine spiritual quality and integrity and they influenced widely a whole generation of their fellow Christians. *(Revd Richard Bevan, Vicar of St Oswald's, Durham 1964-74)*

The Ramseys bought our parents' house at 50 South Street in May 1977 just after my father retired and decided to move on to a smaller house at 34 South Street. The Ramseys' interest was offered by the then Dean, Eric Heaton, a close friend, and a meeting was arranged. The Ramseys came to tea and within a short time expressed interest in buying the house. I still have letters sent by Bishop Michael himself to my father talking about looking at drains etc all of which was done through agents etc but the personal interest and friendship of both Lord and Lady Ramsey was evident from the start.

Eventually they moved in with their faithful housekeeper and friend Audrey Heaton, no relation to the Dean, and her Dandy Dinmont terriers. Calling on them was always a delight and perusing the bookshelves was a particular fascination as the Bishop loved to share his reading interests. We met in South Street at different events and had meals together from time to time. They were still travelling a lot in those days. However he was often seen making his way to the Cathedral wearing his flat cap.

The Ramseys were always interested in the family and after their move to South Bailey in 1979 they urged us to call if we were in Durham. They also called on us when I was living in Devon and then on a visit to Salisbury during one Holy Week. The Bishop was wonderful in company especially when Lady Ramsey was with him. On his own he would be miles away in thought but wonderful to watch!

I remember vividly being asked to collect them to bring them to tea. Strapping the Bishop into car seats in the car took some time as he threw his hands up and roared with laughter at the process. On the journey he sang hymns all the way home. 'When I survey the wondrous cross' was heard several times.

I count it as one of the greatest privileges of my life to have known the Ramseys and think about them often. *(David Surtees)*

At a Founders and Benefactors service in the good old days when it was held on a Wednesday Ramsey attended and so did I. Ramsey in retirement processed with the University and I do not know why, but he did. So I found myself sitting a couple of rows behind him. Come the sermon which was given by a former pupil of his, the preacher went on and on and on such that later services were delayed. *[Brian Crosby was there and timed it: it was 46 minutes—Editor]* Then the preacher said words to the effect that he owed all of the good things in his professional life to the Archbishop sitting below him in the nave.

Then a low, clear, deep growling base voice intoned the following, "I did not teach him to go on as long as this". We heard, we kept solemn. How far did the comment carry—I do not know.

Other than that, passing the unmistakeable figure of the Archbishop in the street I felt that we were living in the presence of a mobile National Monument. And it was a privilege. *(W Barry Woodward)*

My parents arrived in Durham in January 1939 (my father's installation as Canon and Archdeacon was Bishop Hensley Henson's last public event) in a 1927 Humber tourer: it must have been from the Owen household, in which Joan Hamilton was a member and quasi secretary, that my father was seen emerging much muffled and coated; and so he was christened 'Pooh'. To the Ramseys always we have been Mr Paul Pooh, Miss Sarah Pooh etc. Nicknames like this were a frequent part of the Ramsey's private conversation: (Sir) James Duff was 'Willowherb': an incumbent in Sunderland of a particularly earnest persuasion was 'Cum-Cum', pronounced like dum-dum bullets; when his leg was being pulled and at long last the realisation that not all was to be taken at its face value dawned on him, he would say, "Oh come, come". And at Cambridge, Simon Barrington who was 'Actually Sir' as this was the frequent preface to his excuses for not handing in work on time.

Canon Ramsey looked far older than his actually very youthful years. My brother has recorded a version of the story about my father, 25 years his senior, reading his sermon for him in autumn 1939. There had been, according to Hedley Sparkes, a slightly earlier attempt to get him to Durham by creating a new post in the Theology faculty: nothing in fact happened and Ramsey didn't know of this until 1985.

We generally considered that his grasp of practicalities was wanting. Judy Greenslade remembers him learning to ride a bike in The college. Of course as a Cambridge boy and man he was long acquainted with bikes, but was so poor a practitioner that he gave the impression of being a learner. In another field of locomotion, that is processing, we also thought him a poor practitioner as he rolled with his curious sideways progress up Durham's long nave: and I remember seeing Alan Richardson discreetly pointing to his spot when the Canons stood in a quarter circle around the lectern (for perhaps the reading of the ninth lesson at the Christmas Carol services): but this poor showing in processional decorum was reckoned to be less to incompetence or any negative explanation of that kind, than to his mind being on Higher Things, like the Trinity: and so, on balance, it was reckoned to his credit.

We had no garden [the Lucas family lived in what is now the Chorister School — Editor] and so used to play in various spaces close to the house and therefore close to his (their) house. I remember him coming to join me when I was playing soldiers on the lawn beside the Richardson's house: I thought very poorly of his tactical ideas about defence in depth and considered my long, thin red line much preferable. I know that my sister

Sarah, aged 8 or 9 when Ramsey came in 1939, ran races with him in the Monks' Dormitory.

I do not remember our railway being on the top of their house: I do remember it (or rather the permanent outdoor version of it) being in a yard between their house and ours. This impinged on the diocesan office staff, whose offices had been in the laundry of our house. In 1943 the Diocesan Secretary, Mr Carter, complained to me after the surrender of Italy that we were singing the national anthem so often that, with the constantly getting up to stand to attention, his staff were being hindered with their work.

I remember the Ramseys' wedding. It must, I think, be a later memory, not on my part a contemporary one, that they pulled off a considerable coup in announcing their engagement unpredicted and unexpected by the rest of The College. The wedding was in the Galilee Chapel. He wore a cassock: I am sorry to say I cannot remember what Joan wore nor who married them. Probably, therefore, both points fell within my juvenile range of expectations. We—that is to say a dozen or two of both children and adults from The College etc—formed a choir and stood around an upright piano to sing: perhaps it was the choir holidays or perhaps the occasion was designed to be more domestic, less formal than the familiar cathedral occasions. Of course, it was war time and that may have contributed to scale the occasion down: but there was nothing at all about their style which was ever grand.

As my brother has said in his piece, my father was from a decidedly high church tradition: he wore a biretta to go to the Cathedral. The tradition at Durham had been low and public school. Ramsey must have represented an upward shift compared with Oliver Quick, his predecessor. Then in late 1942 the evangelical Sub-Dean, Canon Lillingstone, retired—at last, after 31 years in the post and a sad latter era of indolence and disintegration (see Henson's journal Maundy Thursday and Easter Day 1943). On Boxing Day the Chapter passed a resolution restating the duty of its members to attend Matins (10.00 a.m.) and Evensong (3.00 or 3.30 p.m.) unless otherwise prevented by University or diocesan engagements elsewhere and Canon Mayne, absent through illness, expressly recorded his concurrence at the next meeting.

The Dean, Alington, had been twice Headmaster, at Shrewsbury and Eton, and was an autocrat by nature and experience. With an experienced and exceptionally able Chapter this made for difficulties. On one occasion in Chapter, (I don't know the issue), Ramsey said, "Mr Dean, withdraw". Alington tried to go onto next business. "Mr Dean, withdraw". The same again. And again. "Oh, alright Michael, have it your own way".

Alington had two invaluable means of defusing these situations. The first was his wife—universally agreed to have been one of the most wonderful women, or Christian, anyone you speak to has ever met.

The second was his facility with his pen.

> There was an old Dean who said, "Why
> are my Canons more clever than I",
> They said, "Don't you know?
> You are lazy and low,
> while they are hard working and high."

This particular limerick, though entirely typical of Alington, was in fact a reply to one from Ramsey, who Alington had been pestering for information about the Pelagians. Ramsey himself had written,

> There was a young man who said, "Why
> should I not go to heaven when I die?
> I refuse to believe
> that old Adam & Eve
> can frustrate me if only I try."

Affection and great humour contained differences with great grace.

But there were differences. One of the greatest was about the Ministry. In his lectures Ramsey had referred with approval, before its publication, to Apostolic Ministry: then, on publication, it was reviewed and demolished in a two page article by Canon Claud Jenkins in the 'Church Times'. Nonetheless the stance of this volume was reflected in the Anglo-Catholic opposition to the Church of South India proposals in which Ramsey was active [*The Church of South India, formed in 1947, was an ecumenical Church comprising Anglican, Methodist, Congregational, Presbyterian and Reformed*

Churches—Editor]. By this time, the second half of the 1940, his professional colleague was Greenslade, of Methodist origins and a punctilious historical approach, who contributed to an evangelical collection of essays, 'The Ministry and the Church.' Ramsey reviewed it in 'Theology,' October 1948, trying to fuse the two elements of authority as outlined by Greenslade, essential and ecclesiastical, into a single whole. Greenslade was the standard-bearer for evangelical convictions on the Chapter at that time. Alington was low, in the traditional sense of public schools and colleges, but he had enlivened in the Cathedral and its worship with colour and drama—not within liturgical norms but according to his personal flair. Richardson was SCM, broad and modern, my father Anglo-Catholic and the Bishops of Jarrow certainly above centre but he came as Ramsey was leaving.

> Ah me, how very sad am I,
> just when I thought we'd gottem,
> we lose the ram's truncated eye
> and only keep the bottom. *(Alington)*

In a different quarter, difference was public and robust. Across the river Durham School was presided over by H K Luce, a modernist of rather gloomy hue. Henson had read his commentary on Luke with no enthusiasm one Good Friday in the late 1930s. It was, I think, on the subject of the resurrection that Ramsey did battle with him in the columns of the Times and, to our great satisfaction, upheld the true faith in a vigorous fusillade.

At that time Durham University was very small, only some 500 students, and the Theology faculty had only three staff. Before Ramsey came, Quick, Pace and Sparkes sounded a lively trio. To the small and struggling University the Cathedral made a present of two professors. An Administrative Board did all the administration. So, although the teaching load was wide, the professors were not heavily burdened. Hence Ramsey was able to have more of a ministry in the Church than his successors of today would find possible: he went round the diocese a lot, preaching and teaching, and this made an undoubted base of expectation and welcome for his return as Bishop. I remember his Consecration on Michaelmas Day 1952: we all sailed down to York in the highest spirits and sang 'Stars in the

Morning' with enormous gusto. I recall also how very small indeed the figure of the Bishop-to-be seemed as he stood, in white and alone, in the vastness of York Minster.

In the meanwhile we had got to know them much, much better as they left Durham. They came to stay with us for a few nights over the move: but Joan fell ill with jaundice and stayed five weeks. There is nothing like being ill for getting to know people and for cementing friendships. So, always after this, he was known to us as RP, Reverend Professor, and thus he remained when that stage had receded into the past.

Greenslade, who as the other professorial Canon, was Ramsey's junior colleague for much of his time, was a shy man and blossomed much on Ramsey's removal to Cambridge. A historian of meticulous care, he was infuriated by Alington's slap-dash treatment of facts, like calling Cuthbert's coffin the oldest piece of carved wood in Europe, when it is in fact the second oldest. So apart from considerations of churchmanship and the feeling of being overshadowed, I doubt if he would have found Ramsey's theological approach very companionable. Bishop Henson's reaction to Ramsey's inaugural lecture was kind but distant; he too as a historian could not readily follow Ramsey's very theological style. This letter was written from Henson to Ramsey on 26th March 1941.

> 'My dear Professor,
>
> I am greatly obliged for your inaugural lecture which I have read, if not with complete agreement, perhaps without adequate understanding, but with keen interest and a deep appreciation of its learning, thought and rich suggestiveness.
>
> I think a sound Christian theology must be built on the sure foundation of accurate history. I am rather suspicious of historical study which starts with theological assumptions. But I am not quite sure that I take your true meaning. Anyway, I think you have made an excellent beginning and I cannot doubt that this divinity chair in your hands will be richly serviceable to the church and the university.'

Richardson did a lot in the University in an informal sense and was hard at work on Christian Apologetics and his Theological Word Book of the bible. But he had no University post and may, I suspect, have felt a bit of an outsider on that account, and, I believe, was not happy when Ramsey appointed C K Barrett, a Methodist, onto the faculty. Later, I know that he felt very raw when Ramsey reviewed his 'New Testament Theology' critically, using the word slap-dash of parts of it. Mrs Richardson felt quite envious of Joan Ramsey when the Ramseys went to York, as giving her a completely assured role for the rest of her life.

Both the Richardsons and the Ramseys, of course, were childless. Surely that counted for less, far less, with Michael Ramsey that it has with Hensley Henson. Also, surely his wife counted for more, far more, than with HHH Yet I doubt if there was a direct interconnection. *(The Revd Canon Paul Lucas)*

Michael's writing: I expect you will have some examples that prove just how bad it was *[see page 65 — Editor]* and many a time one of his missives had to be passed around the office staff for as much help as possible for deciphering. Joan's writing was a bit better but very 'flowery'.

Before they moved to 16 South Bailey the flats on the ground and first floors had to be made vacant and then amalgamated to provide suitable accommodation not just for living but for the Bishop's large library. This proved to be so extensive, and heavy, that steel girders had to be inserted under the sitting room on the first floor to take the weight, adding considerably to the contract cost towards which the Ramseys were expected to contribute and I had to negotiate these with Michael. I was led to believe that he was somewhat unworldly but not a bit of it. He knew what he wanted, was as positive about practicalities as many others, especially farmers, that I have had to deal with and what is more, we became quite friendly. Joan was as positive but kept changing her mind about fittings and gave the architect a bit of a run around but on one thing she was absolutely positive, the level of the downstairs sitting room floor.

This floor was in good condition on solid beams but was at a level of about one and a half inches below the hall way and kitchen floors. Joan insisted that the floor must be raised to the level of the others as if things were left as they were she would have great difficulty wheeling in the tea trolley for the Bishop's daily teatime! This seemed to me to be an unnecessary waste of money but she insisted, got her way and if I remember correctly paid for most of the extra cost. What I didn't know was that teatime for Michael was one of the high spots of the day to which he often invited guests: priests, students, visitors to Durham and friends to all of whom he gave love, comfort or advice as required.

There are other stories such as their relationship with Audrey Heaton (no relative of Eric) who had been with them since Lambeth days as a live-in help and did just about everything from cooking, gardening, driving and cleaning and who also kept, bred and showed Dandy Dinmont dogs and was one of the first people I knew who ran a Riding for the Disabled School. It must have been quite a ménage. It was probably the breaking of her good leg and thus the loss of her services which finally persuaded the Ramseys that they would have to leave Durham.

More thoughts on 'M+', as he always signed himself. When he and Joan moved into 16 South Bailey I had a vegetable garden on the other side of his south wall and often had a bonfire—so did the gardeners for that matter. Not wishing to cause any nuisance to the old couple I approached Michael with some diffidence and asked him if he would have any objection. "Not at all," said he, "I love bonfires and will join you when I can with some of my contributions". And he did.

His sermons were special and mostly given extempore because of his poor eyesight in his later years. Just before going to the pulpit he might produce a piece of paper or an old envelope on which he had scribbled a few words to jog his memory but after that it was all 'free speech'.

I expect that you have the couple of books written about Michael just after he died which contain some good stories, e.g. being flooded (twice) by Cyril Watson's washing machine over-flowing from the top flat.

Also, his words on coming down that lovely staircase in 16 South Bailey just before leaving when he said, "This house looks much better without furniture". He and Joan really loved the place and she constantly mentions it in her letters to my wife. And I don't forget her (my dear wife) asking Michael whether he had read all the books in his study to which he replied "most of them"!

A final story: One evening I was getting ready for bed having been out to the pub for a drink. The phone rang. It was Joan, in a panic: Michael had locked himself in the bathroom and was stuck in the bath. I went there and had to hammer the door down. There was then the problem of getting him out of the bath. He was a large man and slippery because he was wet, and it took all my strength to pull him. Eventually I managed to drag him sideways out of the bath and he flopped on the floor like a crab. It was this event which made it obvious that they could no longer continue to live on their own, which is what led to them moving in due course to Bishopthorpe. (*Pat Woodward, formerly Sub Receiver at Durham Cathedral*)

Two policeman were standing in Bishop Auckland market place, one of them was me, a very young policeman, it was Thursday and Market Day. At that time buses used the market place, and Newgate Street was the main road for all traffic. It was a very busy place to be. My senior colleague nudged me and said that someone important wanted to speak to me. I looked over the road to see Michael Ramsey waving at me. Crossing the road, he smiled, asked my name and did I work an early shift every three weeks. Mystified, I said, "Yes," and with a chuckle he said, "That accounts for my early morning tea being late". It had been my practice, when starting at 6.00 a.m. to call at Auckland Castle, visit the Bishop's butler and have a cup of tea with him. "Well, we certainly value your visits to the Castle", he said.

He turned to go, then stopped and said, "I think someone else wants to speak to you". I turned to find the Inspector and the Sergeant watching us. To my surprise they both stood to attention and saluted the Bishop. He walked away, smiling. As I crossed the road, I wondered should I have saluted. The Inspector demanded to know what I had been doing. I explained that the Bishop had thanked me for keeping an eye on the Castle when I was on this beat. "Well, you can keep an eye on it next week," he said. "There is a function and you can see to the car parking". The

Inspector seemed to take great pleasure in making my life a misery! The following week, I was again in trouble, this time involving the local Catholic priest—but that's another story.

Three weeks later I called at the Castle and, on entering, found the Bishop in his dressing gown, having a cup of tea. On my way in, I had met the paper boy and relieved him of the Castle's newspapers. When I removed my cape (yes, policeman wore capes in those days) the Bishop saw the newspapers. "Do you deliver the newspapers as well?" he asked. He took his tea and papers, but on the way out he stopped and asked, "Are you still having trouble with your Inspector?" The butler had been talking!

When Michael Ramsey became Archbishop of Canterbury, I wrote and congratulated him on his preferment. I received a handwritten reply thanking me, with a PS asking if I was looking after the new Bishop.

I last spoke to him in Saddler Street, Durham, near Magdalene Steps. I introduced myself and he immediately started to chuckle. "I certainly did not get the same personal police protection that I received in Durham, when I was at Canterbury" he said. That was the last time I saw or spoke to him before his death.

My first meeting with Bishop Michael was when he confirmed me in St Mary's church at Coxhoe. Although my personal contact with him was brief, I always felt that I was in the presence of a 'Great Man'! *(Douglas Stewart, Ex PC 630 Bishop Auckland Division Durham County Constabulary)*

He never remembered anyone's name but his wife was brilliant at that. Bernard Pawley, later to become Archdeacon of Canterbury, lived in the precincts of Canterbury Cathedral and had two children. Felicity was invited to have tea with the Ramseys. A few days later she was in the Cathedral taking part in a service in which the children had a role, and she saw him in the chancel. He asked, "Where do you live?" Rather than say anything about having tea with him, she simply replied, "In Canterbury." *[Michael de-la-Noy quotes Ramsey's forgetfulness of the names of his nephew and nieces. This is in notable contrast to his ability to remember adults he had met previously—Editor. See de-la-Noy page 106]*

On one occasion when I had spent some time with him a few days earlier, I met him again. Joan said, "You remember Virginia" to which he replied dubiously, "oh, yes, how do you do" [*This story was recounted to me over the phone—the tone of voice was very significant and the implication was that he did not but was playing for time—Editor*]

Chiara Lubich, the founder of the Focalare movement, wanted to meet the Archbishop of Canterbury. He was very apprehensive, "Is she going to preach at me?"

He was brilliant with students. A unique character. (*Virginia Johnstone*)

I first met Michael after a celebration of the Eucharist at Durham University College Chapel just after his election as Bishop. I warmed to him and his eyebrows: at the Prayer for the Church Militant "… and especially for (pause, raised eyebrows, hesitant) Michael our Bishop elect …"

During my sojourn at Sarum Theological College (1952—54) I was invited twice/thrice for lunch at Auckland Castle. After dining we walked in the garden, discussed theology and especially the latest works usually from Germany. His wide and comprehensive book lists, for me, provided my real education. From Durham and York I was privileged to receive handwritten letters as he nurtured me.

I was somewhat amazed when this scholarly, holy ostensibly other-worldly man said, "William if you want to know about the health of a Parish, study the annual accounts on the notice board". "When I visit a Rectory/Vicarage I look into the study to see when the Priest died (i.e. the date of the latest book)."

The last time I met and talked with him was after he retired to Durham (much happier and more settled in Durham than at Cuddesdon); he was on one of his customary walks along the river he loved and he told me he was wrong about 'Honest to God' but didn't share another one of his mistakes for which he had great regret too.

The sermons he preached in the churches of pit villages were simple and easy to understand and yet all the theological nucleus were covered. What a gift! He was a good communicator but silence usually prevailed.

I prepared some members of St Cuthbert's Hebburn Youth Group for confirmation in 1955. One of the candidates was very fashion conscious. He bought a new pair of trousers for the Confirmation but as he was a Teddy Boy they were very tight 'drainpipes'. He suddenly discovered that he couldn't kneel down. Bishop Michael rose to the occasion – stood up and arched those famous eye brows.

I recall one sermon:

"The glory of God as a great cloud filled the temple."
He leans over the pulpit,
"But I can't see a cloud."
Then the eyebrows.
"But the glory of God fills the temple."

He taught me, inspired me, ordained me and nurtured me. I have two heroes/gurus and he is one. I remember him especially for his humility, for example rehearsing for the Coronation Walk (to avoid his rolling tendency), on retirement, "Call me Bishop Michael Ramsey", and his humour e.g. rubbing out a blessing with his hand having inadvertently blessed the water at a Requiem. I also remember Joan's distress when his mitre hit the sanctuary lamp at Chopwell Parish Church and spilt the oil on his 'Coronation Cope'. A truly great man. *(Revd William Armstrong)*

I am a member of Elm Ridge Methodist Church in Darlington. We were delighted to have the Bishop with us on the bi-centenary day for our Church in 1953. *[The programme shows the information: Tuesday 26ᵗʰ May 1953, Public meeting at 7.00 p.m. Speakers The Bishop of Durham, Dr AM Ramsey, Revd Dr Maldwyn Edwards and Mrs Clifford Towlson, MA (Leeds). Chairman Mr J Berriman. Editor.]* His graciousness shone through the proceedings and his timely words were an inspiration. The singing, with a packed church, was great. My father was organist for the occasion.

In the 1960s I lived in Manchester. During the Week of Prayer for Christian Unity we met, on two occasions, at the Free Trade Hall. The first time Cardinal Heenan was the preacher. The following year Michael Ramsey, as Archbishop of Canterbury. Some of us were privileged to attend the reception afterwards at Manchester Town Hall. When I met the Archbishop I referred to the bi-centenary meeting. Without hesitation he straightway gave the full date. How amazing! *(Mrs Kath Adams)*

In around 1955, while I was Curate-in-charge of the Church of Springwell St Mary, Sunderland, I was considering a move to a new parish. My wife Dinah and I went to look at a church in Middlesbrough (in the diocese of York), but for various reasons decided against it. I reported this to Bishop Ramsey who sympathised with my decision remarking that, "Those who go to York go to the bad!" This turned out to have been a joke against himself; he must already have known at the time that he was about to make his own move to York, as Archbishop. *(The Revd Canon Colin Purvis)*

Michael Ramsey with The Revd Canon Colin Purvis and a confirmation candidate at St Mary's Church, Springwell, Sunderland
(Photo courtesy of the Revd Canon Colin Purvis)

We met the Ramseys when they became our neighbours in South Street. We didn't see a lot of them, we sometimes chatted in the garden and Joan and I had coffee together occasionally, but Michael didn't join us. During the first winter there they realised that walking to the Cathedral was not so easy and Michael fell a few times, so they decided to ask at the Cathedral if there was anywhere closer they could live. They moved to South Bailey and we continued to see each other socially. *(Mrs Joy Gazzard)*

My son Tom was at the Chorister School and a batch of confirmand lads including him were confirmed by Michael Ramsey who was already retired and had moved up from Oxford to Durham. He came into the Cathedral very extendedly coped and had bushy hair and bushy eyebrows and very much impressed the young confirmands. *(Mr Robin Dower)*

I was confirmed when I was a very young boy by Michael Ramsey. It must have been 1953, I guess. Just before the Coronation of our Queen. The only thing I can remember was being told by our local vicar not to wear Brylcream, as Dr Ramsey would get his hands sticky. *(Professor Peter Fawcett)*

I was with George Zealley (alto lay clerk, 1947-69) approaching the slype door, when he was spotted by Archbishop Michael who had come north to attend a funeral in the Cathedral. MR not only recognised him, but without any prompting he asked after Ann and Pam (George's wife and daughter) as well.

I remember too the day his retirement was announced. The choir was assembled in the slype ready for Evensong when we were told that after the service we would be going by "bus to Newcastle", because the Archbishop had requested that as part of the announcement on the 6:00 News we would sing *Ave verum corpus*, his favourite anthem. I cannot recall whether it was the setting by Dvořák or Mozart, but I do remember the driver getting lost twice, and us arriving at Newcastle to find an anxious Mike Neville waiting for us. As there was not time for him to explain the choreography to Richard Lloyd and for Richard to take us through the anthem, much to MN's astonishment we practised it on our own. (*A former member of the Cathedral choir*)

I was confirmed by Michael Ramsey in 1953 in my home town of Stanley. I can still remember his text: "Blessed are they that dwell in thy house, they will be alway praising thee." An amazing man. We were all somewhat in awe of this imposing medieval looking person in episcopal garb. We teenagers were also amused to discover (I think I've got this right) that he and Cary Grant were the same age or possibly even shared a birthday. A greater contrast could not be imagined.

Many years later when I was vicar of St Mark's, Millfield in Sunderland I attended the 50th anniversary in Shildon of the ordination of Hugh Corden who was then vicar of Shildon. This must have been in the early 1980s.

There was a large gathering and we were told there was to be a special guest. As I waited to join the throng in the hall a car arrived and out got the special guest—Michael Ramsey. He had retired some years before. He spoke to me as we waited to get into the hall and asked where my parish was. So I said, "St Mark's, Millfield". He replied "Ah yes. Arthur Pugh used to be vicar there." Here was proof of his reputation for having an amazing memory. Arthur Pugh had been vicar of St. Mark's in the 50s or 60s. Michael Ramsey had been Archbishop of York and Canterbury since those days in the Durham Diocese.

One more little story. I remember being told that during his time as Archbishop of Canterbury he was known to wander round the Cathedral and would sometimes tap a visitor on the shoulder and say, "You don't know me but I'm the Archbishop of Canterbury." I don't know what the reaction was. I think he was a good person for the role of Archbishop at a time when the repercussions of 'Honest to God' were being felt throughout the church. As a theologian of depth he understood the issues better than some of the clergy I knew who wanted him to condemn John Robinson's writings. (*The Revd Peter D. Atkinson*)

Soon after I moved to Durham Cathedral in 2005, I spent a few days fulfilling a prior commitment to give some lectures at Nashotah House in Wisconsin, the seminary where the Ramseys spent considerable amounts of time in their retirement. As soon as people there heard I was at Durham, they too started to tell me stories about him. One, in particular, stands out in my mind. He had gone for a walk in the surrounding countryside—low rolling hills in which buildings were set without fences. Nearby, a psychiatric residential care home had lost one of their elderly male residents and the police had been alerted. They were searching the countryside and came upon a white haired, elderly gentleman:

"Hello, sir. We've been looking for you."
"I'm not lost. I'm just taking a walk."
"Come along with us and we'll take you home."
"Do you know who I am? I'm the former Archbishop of Canterbury'"
"Yes, sir. They all say that. Now come along with us."

Someone from Nashotah House had to go and rescue him and explain to the police that this really was the retired Archbishop of Canterbury. *(The Revd Canon Rosalind Brown)*

When Michael Ramsey had retired from the office of Archbishop of Canterbury, he used regularly to visit the Anglican seminary of Nashotah House, Wisconsin, where he was very popular. Nashotah stands on a lake, and Michael liked to walk round the lake for an afternoon's outing. On the opposite side of the lake to the seminary there was a lunatic asylum, to which Michael was noticed to give a very wide berth. When asked the reason, he replied: "If I were to go into that place, and they asked me who I was, and I said I was the former Archbishop of Canterbury, they would never let me out!" *(Professor Gerald Bonner)*

When I was appointed to the staff of Lincoln Theological College, Eric Abbot, my spiritual director who had been the Warden of Lincoln, told me he had given Michael Ramsey, the Sub-Warden, a report on the training of clergy in the Church of England. At breakfast the following day Eric Abbot asked him what he thought? "It is very good", Ramsey replied, "but I think it under-estimates the theatrical ability of many Anglican clergy and their capacity for mimicry."

When I arrived in Lincoln in January 1983 Michael Ramsey had made a recent visit. At the end of the day he gave an address in the chapel at which he said:

"When I die and arrive at the gates of heaven and St Peter enquires as to who I am, I shall say, 'Ramsey, Arthur Michael, sometime Sub-Warden of Lincoln Theological College'. I look at those of you training for ordination today, with your computers and all the advantages of modern living, and say to myself, 'Michael, had you lived in these times, you might have gone far.'" *(The Revd Nicholas Holtam)*

It was 65 years ago in September 1945 that I and four other ten year old boys arrived at Durham Cathedral Chorister School to start our first term as boarders in the immediate aftermath of the Second World War. The most eccentric of the clergy, as seen through the eyes of a choirboy not yet in his teens, was undoubtedly Canon Michael Ramsey who, from 1940-50, was both a Canon of the Cathedral and also Professor of Divinity at Durham University.

I remember Canon Ramsey as an imposing figure of a man, bald headed but with an abundance of white hair atop his long white surplice and looking for all the world like a biblical patriarch, old beyond his years: he cannot then have been much over 40 but he looked almost twice that age that he did on television in June 1963 when as Bishop of Durham he attended the Queen at her coronation in Westminster Abbey. However it was his custom when walking in procession through the Cathedral with the choir and other clergy at Durham to stride ahead at the same time gazing heavenwards with arms folded across his upper chest just below the chin, thinking lofty thoughts, no doubt, or simply drawing inspiration from the awesome surroundings.

It was customary at the great choral service over Christmas for the vergers to light all the candles on the two massive chandeliers suspended over the choir stalls. Draughts blowing around the Cathedral were such that on that occasion the melted wax from one or two of the candles dropped onto the predominantly white marble floor between *Decani* and *Cantoris* [*the two sides of choir—Editor*].

On one such occasion Canon Ramsey, lurching heavy-footed down the steps from his stall behind the choir gentlemen, joined the other clergy processing up to the high altar. Head held high and arms folded across his chest, there was no prospect of his spotting the danger ahead of him on the marble floor; but as one we choristers spotted the inevitable outcome of the drama about to unfold before us. Sure enough Canon Ramsey stepped on some of the fallen wax and lost his balance as his foot slipped away from beneath him. The choristers to a boy expected him to fall but by some miracle he was able to recover and continued on his way to the altar as though nothing untoward had occurred.

The boys on either side could not suppress a broad grin for which we received a sound ticking off from our Headmaster in the vestry the moment the service was over. Cathedral choristers, as we well knew, were not supposed to show any emotion!

On another occasion the choir and clergy were in procession through the Cathedral singing the Litany unaccompanied under the direction of the Choirmaster at the start of Sunday morning service. That Sunday morning we processed from the under clock through the South Transept towards the Crossing beneath the central tower as we did most days when taking the short route to our places in the Chancel.

But, being the Litany, we took a left turn down the nave side aisle to the font and then up the centre aisle to the Crossing and thence to our stalls. On arriving in the Chancel we choristers immediately spotted that Canon Ramsey, who had been following us in the line of clergy at the rear of the procession, was already in his stall, a look of utter confusion on his face as he realised that he must have left the procession by mistake as it turned into the side aisle and walked straight ahead on his own from the Transept to his seat in the Chancel!

Although these anecdotes provided the boys and even some of the choir men with rare opportunities for mirth-making, it would be fair to say that Canon Ramsey was well loved during his time at Durham. I particularly recall one of the annual Miners' Gala Services when the Cathedral was packed with miners and their families from the surrounding pit villages. Durham was closed to traffic for the day as the miners assembled on the Racecourse with their colourful Lodge banners to be addressed by the leading Labour politicians of the day. In the afternoon many of the miners and their families made their way to the Cathedral accompanied by their brass bands. The Cathedral was full to the doors: standing room only as it always was for Miners' Gala.

The sermon that year was preached by Canon Ramsey. Although Professor of Divinity he spoke in simple straightforward terms and while I cannot now remember a word of what he said, I do remember that in the packed Cathedral you could have heard a pin drop as this saintly man addressed the congregation. And then the service ended with the organ and the brass bands at maximum volume, each trying to outdo the other for the final hymn; and the vergers wondering how to clear the Cathedral before the next day's service of all the helium-filled coloured balloons released by the children during the service and floating upwards to end up bobbing about under the vaulted roof! (*David V. Evans*)

I knew Bishop Michael from 1978 until his death. He moved to the Bailey around the time I went to Chad's in 1978 where he had a number of theology students to his home regularly for seminars; his humility was huge—I remember the subject of the Sacred Heart of Jesus coming up at one of these seminars and he was rather dismissive of this devotion and, rather foolishly I blurted out, "But it's not like that at all". "Oh, do inform us Carl, do inform us" came the response; although I wanted the ground to swallow me up I came to realise very quickly that he meant it not as a put-down but as a genuine question about his thirst to learn more. A similar incident happened when I once came across him in the library of St Stephen's House; he was making a huge tower of books and muttering to himself. I crept closer and, before he saw me I heard what he was muttering—"So much to read, so much to learn; so much to read, so much to learn". I was encouraged by the thought that the 100th Archbishop of Canterbury was still learning in his 80's and that clearly meant there was hope for me.

Father Michael (which was something he loved being called in the USA and at his beloved Nashotah House) was extremely affectionate and seemed to spend a great deal of energy on the relationships he had with those younger than himself; one always felt that he was truly interested even in the trivia which often seemed to fill our lives at Durham. When I was accepted for ordination to the priesthood he regularly made time to see me on my own and encouraged me to think about my prayer-life and how I would keep a discipline of prayer going in a busy parish. He knew I was from East Hull—a pretty rough parish near the docks—and I discovered his phenomenal memory; he could remember not only who was parish priest there when he was Archbishop of Canterbury but also the names of the churchwardens! I asked him once what were his priorities when he was a bishop. He didn't hesitate in his reply, "first my priests, then my ordinands, then my churchwardens". I guess this was all before bishops became bogged down by administration and the number of staff and clergy available to the parishes was much greater. We discussed the suggestion by ACCM [the Advisory Council for the Church's Ministry—Editor] I spend a year out before going to St Stephen's House—after all I was only 19 when I was accepted for training and the then, Bishop of Hull wanted me to go and work in a factory in Birmingham. Having grown up in East Hull and worked in factories during vacations I was not particularly pleased. I told Bishop Michael and he agreed—in fact, he told me, "it will be quite immoral for you to take a job that someone else actually needs simply to broaden your experience. No, Carl, God wants you to be a priest and so you need to learn about being a priest." We talked about having a two year gap before training and he promptly wrote to the Bishop of Chicago, Jim Montgomery, the Dean of Milwaukee, James Leech, and the Dean of Nashotah House to see what they could do. A few weeks later I was having a rather lazy morning when I heard a commotion on the stairs near my room in Grads. "Carl, Carl, Carl" then there was a hammering on the door; I opened it and Bishop Michael laughed his usual laugh and said, "oh, I have got you out of bed, I have got Carl out of bed!" He then shared his news that I was able to spend two years at All Saints Cathedral, Milwaukee, and invited me to come and discuss it in his study, "when you are dressed". Off he went, chuckling and he delighted in embarrassing me at drinks parties both here and in America by saying, "I remember when the Archbishop of Canterbury got Carl out of bed!"

I remember serving mass for him many times—I think his regular day was a Tuesday—and I am sure people have repeated ad-nauseam the story about not blessing the water. What I remember was the way he used to pick up the altar missal to read the words. He held it so close to his eyes. I was moved to think how poor his eye-sight was until someone remarked that, as the dominical words hadn't really changed since they had been first written down it was probably more his mischievousness.

Once when I was having lunch with him he was showing some papers from Pope Paul VI in his study when there was a terrible commotion outside. We went to the window and saw the most ridiculous sight—there was Lady Ramsey and Audrey (his housekeeper) trying to wield the largest pick-axe I have ever seen. "Ah, they are gardening" said Michael.

At a drinks party I once remarked to Lady Ramsey that, "I have never called Bishop Michael 'my Lord'" "Well, there's always plenty of time to start Carl" came the reply.

Once when I was at Little St Mary's, Cambridge, someone told me the story of how Michael had taken away the low mass vestments from Lambeth Palace when Donald Coggan became Archbishop and returned them when Runcie was enthroned. I asked him about that and he confirmed that they had sneaked them away, "We rather thought, we rather thought that the Cog would turn them into cushion covers!" he said and guffawed. He often talked about 'The Cog' but he was always deferential. Lady Ramsey was not quite so restrained and, when Robert Runcie was made Archbishop of Canterbury she said to me, "It is so nice to have an Archbishop that is more of an Archbishop than his wife". (I'm not really sure if that's a good thing to print!).

They came to see me several times while I was in the States and he stayed at Nashotah House. We used to go for walks by the lake and he told me stories of his life as a bishop and then as Archbishop of both York and Canterbury. He was very coy about the Royal Family but did share one or two stories which made him smile, particularly in relation to the power of the Queen being curtailed. He was fond of the Queen Mother, "a good Scottish Episcopalian" he said and was very amused by Princess Margaret's visits to Deptford. He was not so complimentary about Prince Philip but thought Prince Charles earnest and sincere. He took to riding an exercise bike whilst he was Nashotah House; "Don't you find it dull?" I said, "No, Carl, no" he said, "I pretend that I am Archbishop of York and I ride across the Plain of Holderness and through Pickering and into the North Yorkshire Moors—up and down and up and down".

The Dean arranged a birthday party for me one year and we went to the best restaurant in Milwaukee. After Perier Jouet Champagne at the Deanery we went to the private dining room and a splendid meal with a beef dish created for the occasion and, afterwards, named by the German Executive Chef Filet de boeuf 'Canterbury'. It was very lovely and extravagant—Michael Ramsey was not impressed—"I would have been happy with a sandwich" he said.

I remember one Sunday evening we had Solemn Evensong and Benediction at the Cathedral and Bishop Michael preached a powerful and urgent sermon on the real presence. His text was 'And when I am lifted up from the earth I shall draw all things to myself'. In hushed tones and with a packed cathedral where you could hear a pin drop he said, "In a moment, the Blessed Sacrament will be placed on the altar, and we shall adore the presence of Christ—lifted up he will draw all things to himself".

He went to the Episcopal Church Center once in 5th Avenue, New York City, and was surprised to find himself at a mass presided over by a woman. "What did you do?" I said. "What did you think I would do?" came the reply, "I stayed of course but I hope no one finds out!"

When I returned from the States I stayed with him and he brought me tea and biscuits on a tray in the morning, "Ah, the Archbishop wakes up Carl again!" he said—and went away chuckling. He noticed that I had clearly had a good look through his spare wardrobes where I found his clerical evening coats and other ridiculous items; "Did you find anything that fits dear Carl?" he chuckled as he went out of the room.

He came to visit at St Stephen's House, Oxford, twice while I was there, and then moved to St John's home. We had a fire-work party one evening and he sat with Lady Ramsey in a rather grand chair watching the display. One large Catherine wheel was not nailed to the post very well and suddenly shot off and rolled towards him; ordinands rushed to save him and someone threw a bucket of water on the Catherine wheel. All the while he was chuckling away. "Father," I said, "you could have been burnt to death like Cranmer" "I like to choose my own company" he said with a glint in his eye.

We had a tradition at Staggers [St Stephen's House—Editor] of gathering in a particular room for a coffee immediately after breakfast. We used to have fads and the latest fad when Michael and Lady Ramsey came was knitting! There we were, several of us knitting scarves ... I remember Martin Warner and Andrew Walker being there (both Chadsmen) and we were listening to some music as we talked. Someone commented on it and Lady Ramsey, who disliked background music said rather tartly, "Well, it's rather like being in a Harrods' lift!". There was a knock at the door and a member of staff came in—I think it was Fr Franklin—who disliked anything camp or exotic. "Look at you—sitting here and drinking coffee and knitting when you should be studying," (he hadn't see Michael and Lady Ramsey sandwiched between people on the sofa) "Oh, I am very sorry, I am very sorry" said Bishop Michael and promptly got up to leave! He turned and gave us a wonderful smirk!

I have a large number of letters from him, some of them containing lovely lines of wisdom—like the time I asked his advice on testing my vocation to the religious life. I just opened one and there is a comment from him from October 1982: "The Durham term starts today; and the Bailey is swimming with students. On Saturday there is to be an Orthodox-Anglican conference, starting with a High Mass celebrated by me in St Chad's, and ending with Orthodox Vespers. I will send you more news when the term has settled down". It warmed my heart to hear all these little snippets of Durham life coming from him—he regularly wrote and telephoned to tell me 'Durham News'—he loved Durham and students gave him a wonderful quality of life.

I have some nice pictures of him somewhere—with Chadsmen and at Nashotah House and Staggers—surrounded by students. I also have a fabulous one of him in choir dress outside 'Michael' the Nashotah House bell during the fall. He used to appear at lectures in Nashotah House—just walk in—and disrupt them a little—I am sure he knew exactly what he was doing but he loved pretending that he didn't. He used to tease the Nashotah House seminarians and ask them to say the word 'wrath'—he would mimic them and laugh till he cried. *(The Revd Canon Carl Turner)*

My memories are mainly about Joan. She was an excellent correspondent and her humour and chattiness made up for Michael's silences. They were both grateful for any small kindnesses, and effusive in their thanks.

They lived first of all in South Street, buying the house from Paddy and Bill Surtees who moved to a smaller house in South Street. When the journey over the river by foot became too much for them, they moved to 16 South Bailey.

Audrey Heaton (no relation to Eric Heaton) was the Ramsey's cook and help. She was often seen wearing her apron going along the Bailey with her beloved dog at her side. She had a slight limp, which did not seem to deter her in any way. She had answered an advert for a cook and left Penrith to work at Lambeth Palace for Archbishop Fisher around 1958. The Ramseys took her on when they arrived and she was with them until they moved from Durham. She used to invite The College children in via the tradesman's entrance in the Bailey to see her 'dolls house' inhabited by little mice figures. She was always very kind and friendly.

The last time I saw Joan Ramsey was at the Miners' Gala. She was sitting on Magdelene Steps with the general public, watching the bands and banners go by, she loved to be with the Durham people as an equal.

When they attended the Cathedral they didn't expect any special treatment and joined the congregation sitting wherever there was a place, often on the Dean's side in the choir when the congregation used to sit up there before the coming of the nave altar.

We entertained the Ramseys at 13 The College, and it was at lunch that they told us the sausage and mash story. Alexander their butler at Auckland Castle thought sausage and mash was too 'infra dig' and so didn't serve it. Until Michael said in his hearing that he had very much enjoyed sausage and mash at the House of Lords. Thereafter it was on the menu!

Joan worked for Bishop Owen at number 15 The College (his daughter Faith was Joan's bridesmaid and we met Faith when we lived in Winchester, she attended our Church of St Cross). At that time number 13 was part of number 15 and Joan remembers the maid standing at the top of the dining room steps of number 13 in wartime holding up a dish cloth which was very holey saying, "give me the tools and I'll finish the job."

I thought if I let you see Joan's letters they would show her delightful character. Gordon Hopkins with whom Denis lived in Pallion when we met, was a great friend of the Ramseys. Michael and he had been in Liverpool together. After Gordon retired as a Canon of Durham he lived in Prebends' Gatehouse (where we now live) so we have known this house ever since. Joan remembered the days when 'Miss Jopling', later Mrs Box, lived at the Gatehouse and opened the gate for those allowed through. Mrs Box was here when we first came to Durham in 1975. I love the phrase 'clarting about' — a real northern word — which Joan used when imagining Michael and Gordon in heaven.

Denis represented the Durham Chapter at Joan's funeral in Canterbury. *(Mrs Val Trigg)*

I remember two occasions on which Bishop Ramsey visited St Chad's College during my undergraduate years.

On the first occasion, probably 1955, he spoke of his long and loving association with Durham and in terms which he left us with more than just an impression that he would be happy to spend the rest of his ministry in the diocese.

On his second visit, in the following year, after the translation to York had been announced, he was mindful of, or was reminded of, what he had previously said about his attachment to Durham. His comment, delivered with beaming smile, was, "All I can say is, in the words on the Psalmist, Put your trust not in Princes!" *(Dr Michael Boyd)*

Early in 1954 I received a letter from the Bishop's Chaplain asking me to go to see the Bishop. I was in my second year at Cambridge, reading Theology, having been accepted for the ministry first by Bishop Alwyn Williams and then by CACTM *[Central Advisory Council for the Ministry — Editor]*. But Bishop Michael Ramsey had not met me. So in the Easter vacation I went to be interviewed at Auckland Castle. The Bishop answered the door to me and took me to his study. After some conversation he asked me how I had done in the exams at the end of my first year. I said that as I had had to learn both Greek and Hebrew from scratch, and I had found that difficult, I had not done very well. At the mere idea of anyone finding those subjects a problem his versatile eyebrows nearly rose to his hairline. He surveyed the ceiling and then, stuttering a little commented, "Well, we must aspire upwards."

He then asked whether I would like to see his chapel. It seemed only polite to say that I would. As he led me across the drive from the study to the chapel he explained that in Mediaeval times the chapel had been a banqueting hall. I responded that I had not known the bishops had been at Bishop Auckland in Mediaeval days. He put his arm round my shoulder and said, "My dear boy, the Bishops of Durham have lived at Bishop Auckland since before the Norman Conquest!" Unfortunately, by the time I was ordained in 1958 he was Archbishop of York, and my ordaining Bishop was Maurice Harland.

My second meeting with him was at tea following a celebration of an anniversary of Lincoln Theological College, where he had once been a member of the staff. As I was going in, the Warden, Alan Webster, (no relation) took my arm and said, "Go and sit at the Archbishop's right, there is an empty place there." So I gathered my two slices of bread and a mug of tea and went where I had been told. I told the Archbishop that I was under orders to keep him company, and that I was David Webster, and had been the Curate at Billingham St Cuthbert's. "Yes, yes, Canon Tymms' old church. I have been to see him, you know." "Yes, I know, the Canon told me so when I visited him at Dulverton Hall in Scarborough."

After a little conversation with the others the Archbishop turned to me and said, "You did something in the interregnum, didn't you?" I replied that I had looked after the parish during an interregnum of 18 months, but did nothing that hit the headlines. He could not recall what it was, then after a while he turned to me and said, "Billingham Parish Magazine, an exhortation on Christian unity." "Well, yes," I replied, "I did write the Vicar's letter during the interregnum, and in January, thinking of the Week of Prayer for Christian Unity, I might well have written about it. But I didn't think it was remarkable." The Archbishop replied, "Well, I remarked it." That was perhaps six to eight years later, and he was able to recall a vicar's letter in a parish magazine, and who had written it.

I had no further meetings with Michael Ramsey, but years later, after his death, when Pat and I were on holiday in Oxford, we went to visit Mrs Ramsey. She was delighted to have someone to talk to about Durham and its people. She was by then very frail, and died, I think a couple of years later.

No one is more deserving of a window in Durham Cathedral than Michael, and we plan to be there when it is dedicated. *(The Revd David Webster)*

My associations with Archbishop Ramsey arose from my long connection with Second Commander John Lawrence-Owen who was the son of Bishop Owen who had been Bishop of Jarrow and subsequently became Bishop of Lincoln. The Bishop had married Archbishop Ramsey.

Mrs Owen had been widowed, her husband having died in the early 1960s. She was in the habit of entertaining the clergy on alternative Sundays. One Sunday I was fortunate to meet Archbishop Ramsey there and we were talking about John Lawrence-Owen and he looked rather bewildered. Then Mrs Owen left us to prepare supper. He said to me, "I don't think I know of whom you are speaking." I said, "I am talking about John Lawrence-Owen who was the son of Bishop Owen." The Bishop then looked rather puzzled and said, "You know I don't know him." I commented that the name 'Lawrence' could be used as a surname or a Christian name. He asked, "Does he hyphenate the 'Lawrence Owen'?" I said I didn't know. There was a long pause, then he said, "If it is hyphenated it implies they weren't married. You must tell him to discontinue its use." Many years later when John Lawrence-Owen and I were serving together I lent him a book. When he returned the book there was a postcard in it which I still have and I noticed that Lawrence-Owen was hyphenated.

One day during the rehearsal for the Coronation it was bucketing down with rain. Security had been stepped up and people were being checked as they came in. Bishop Ramsey arrived in from the pouring rain. One of the younger vergers was at the door and asked him who he was. The Bishop opened his great coat slowly and said in a low voice, "I am the Bishop of Durham". The Verger was completely taken aback and exclaimed, "Gawd, My Lord!"

Once Sunday evening I stayed with the Ramseys after one of the Coronation rehearsals which I had had to attend. We were drinking tea after supper—I don't think he drank much coffee. He had dribbled the tea and Mrs Ramsey jumped up very quickly and it up, telling me, "If ever he does that, you must clean it up." At the next rehearsal there was a break and I collected some tea for the Bishop. When I returned he was in conversation with the Bishop of London. I suddenly noticed he'd spilled something on the front of his cassock so I quickly ran across and rubbed it off with my handkerchief. The Bishop of London looked very alarmed so I said, "My Lord, I've been ordered to see to you."

There was a famous occasion at one rehearsal when the Bishop was late. This was reported widely but I don't think it ever bore much evidence of the truth. Suffice to say he had mixed up the time of the rehearsal with an appointment he had made to have his hair cut. Everything started and it was said that the Queen was extremely annoyed. To cut a long story short, when he arrived he had obviously spoken to her and I saw that she smiled nicely at him and that was that.

There was also the story of when he was invited to, I think, Balmoral. During a party game everyone was asked to write or draw their first association on hearing a phrase. In response to 'Hark, hark the lark' Bishop

Ramsey drew in the left hand corner of the piece of foolscap paper a lark with large ears. *[A similar story that was recounted to me is that, at a New Year's House party with the Royal Family, people were told what to draw for the others to guess. Princess Margaret told Michael Ramsey that he was to draw 'The bosom of Abraham'.—Editor]*

Very early in the rehearsals for the Coronation, the Queen's Principal Naval Aide de Camp told me that we ought to know the various people and he had reason to believe that before the rehearsal sitting quietly on the south side of the High Altar was the Archbishop, and the Bishop sitting on the left was the Bishop of London. I replied, "I think it's Bishop of Durham." He said to me, "How do you know that?" and I said "I suppose I must have seen them in 'Tatler' or in the 'News of the World'." The Admiral then said to me, "I'm sure it's the Bishop of London. You go and ask him who he is and I'll approach the Archbishop." So I went to Bishop Ramsey and said to him, "The Admiral has reason to believe that you are the Bishop of London." "No, no, no" he said, standing tall, "In the context of this place and for these purposes, I am the Bishop of Durham." *(Surgeon Captain RN (Rtd) Robert Etherington).*

Michael Ramsey lectured the diploma in theology students in the gospels and doctrine, but his habit was to start lecturing before he got into the lecture room, he carried on lecturing through the period and then concluded the lecture as he was leaving the room. He was a very popular lecturer because you could actually take down every word he said in long hand because he went that slowly and he was very popular with the students indeed. *(A member of the clergy)*

I went to work with Michael Ramsey in the autumn of 1967 where I became his radio and television officer and initially, he being a very shy man, it took me nine months sitting in the back of his Daimler to actually get him to talk to me. Eventually I said to him, "I went to the International New Testament Conference in Oxford two years ago and you were doing a piece on Bultmann *[a New Testament scholar—Editor]* and you absolutely demolished Bultmann." From then on, I never had any trouble talking to

Michael Ramsey: as far as he was concerned I could talk theology and that meant that anything was worth discussing so long as it was theology. But try to talk to Michael about anything else: he had no small conversation and no small talk at all.

At the end of that year he was doing a New Year's Eve message in the city of London and I suppose we didn't clear out of the city until after midnight because he said, "Well look, you come back to Lambeth with me at this late hour of the night and we'll put you up." So we got to Lambeth and there was nobody in the Palace except Joan and Michael. Joan asked me if there was anything I would like and I said, "To be quite honest, I just want a glass of cold water." Joan walked around the palace for 15 minutes trying to find cold water and eventually came back saying, "I've no idea where there is a cold water tap." She added, "I will always remember you as the man who wanted cold water in the middle of the night." So I went up to the bedroom they had given me and there was a whole batch of Lambeth Palace notepaper so I said to myself, "Well, this is the one occasion when I can really enjoy myself" so I wrote four different letters to friends of mine who were all clergy. It was only size A5 note paper, so I wrote 'Dear Smith, or Brown' or whatever the names were, 'It gives me the very greatest pleasure to offer you', and then over the page, 'my very good wishes, Michael, but not the right one'. So some of my friends were not best pleased about that.

He hadn't been very good at broadcasting and so I said to him "Come to the television centre where they train people." "Oh yes" he said he would do this. So I took him out to BBC Television Centre at Shepherd's Bush and I said in the meantime to the other trainees, all of whom were Methodist minsters, "What I want from you more than anything else is an absolute honest answer and straight piece of how Michael Ramsey does on television." They said "We wouldn't do anything other than that, we're Methodists." So we went with him and they didn't make one critical comment in half an hour, they flattered him and flannelled him. As he and I went out in the car I said, "I always think of that lot as Methodist Aunties." He laughed and said, "Ha, ha, ha, ha. I like, like it, like it. Methodist aunties, Methodist aunties."

One of the things that was understood by those of us who work in Church House was that whatever happened you must never ever ask Joan Ramsey to change an arrangement for a room that had been booked for something. I was due to arrange for him to do a broadcast for BBC and when I got there she had allocated me a completely white room. Now this was just after they had arranged all the colour TV. I walked in and looked at it and said, "I know what will happen, as soon as we get there the BBC producers will said that "there is absolutely no way that we will do this broadcast if it is all white on the wall.'" I said, "Give me a few minutes". So I thought what I do, thinking if I ask Joan to change it, all the rules say that she will kick me out and I will lose my job. The only thing I can do is seriously attempt to seduce her. It is difficult to imagine Joan and Michael making love, it is just not part of the package. So when she came into the room I effectively tried to seduce her—not in a sensual way but emotionally: and I got the room. I never had any more trouble with her at all and I think this is because I treated her as a woman. I don't think Michael ever treat her as a woman, he just wasn't that sort of man.

He and I were going up Whitehall in the Daimler, we'd just past the Cenotaph and for some reason or other he started talking about how fed up he was with the evangelical Bishops who were in the General Synod because, "you can nnnever nnnever get them to commit themselves to anything." As we went on something came up about John Stott *[then Rector of All Souls, Langham Place –Editor]* came up in the conversation who was a great friend of mine. He said, "Stott, Stott, Stottttt. Such an intransigent man, such an intransigent man." I said "Archbishop, you really cannot have it both ways. You want people who will stand up and be counted and when John Stott does that you don't want to know." Then in 1969 Maurice Wood was appointed Bishop of Norwich and I commented that the evangelical priests were very pleased with the appointment. "Yes, yes" he said, "but how long will it be before they repudiate him?" And so I laughed about that with him. Then later that day when we were coming back from wherever we had been he said "Mmmmmmorris Wood, not I think a *very* great brain."

When they retired, they moved to a house in South Bailey and they invited me to go and have lunch. So I came from London and sat down for lunch and they provided me with a very nice main course. When I had finished the main course, he got up, all dressed in black—jet black—and said, "Would you like some more?" I said, "That is very kind of you." So he came over and plonked food on my plate and then turned around and fell over and literally fell on his back. He was lying there like a black beetle with his feet and arms and legs in the air and couldn't move. Joan and I ran over and grabbed one end each desperately trying to get him off the ground. We did succeed eventually but that was really quite an achievement. *(The Revd Canon Michael Saward)*

What I remember about Michael Ramsey is that he had a stammer, but we ignored that, and also his remembrance of who people were and where they had ministered even though he might have seen them in a completely different context, and his care. Whenever I met him he always asked how I was and I think it was the personal touch that he had which was very marked. And his interests in what people were doing in their ministry, how they felt about their ministry and if there was anything that he could do to help further which didn't very often happen. And seeing him in action in a parish for example both Ryhope and St Andrew's, Roker, Sunderland; I remember him coming there for confirmation and the way he went round and talked to the families of the newly confirmed afterwards. I know some people thought that he wasn't that sort of a person, but in a pastoral situation he knew what it was all about and I think a lot of people gained from him just speaking to them because the Bishop is sort of 'up there' in some people's eyes. He really made a point of talking to people and listening to people which doesn't always go together. And if people talked about something he wasn't sure of, he wasn't shy in saying, "Can you tell me a bit more? Can you broaden it out?" I think it was his pastoral ministry to one and all that was tremendous because a lot of people I think felt in awe of him and that was partly because of his size, I suppose. But once they got to know him and he would go and talk to them after confirmation when you went into the hall to have a cuppa he would go around, particularly to the parents and the candidates and that for me also said what a good shepherd he was. He loved people.

Occasionally he talked about somebody, giving them the wrong name. You knew he wasn't talking about that person at all, but he wasn't always very good at ascribing what he was talking about into the right person. But was humble enough to accept his error if you said to him, "Was that not somebody else?" *(The Revd Margaret Parker)*

My late dear wife Bessie Billingham was secretary of St Chad's from 1960-84 of which Canon John Fenton Oxford used to say, "Bessie you are worth more than five tutors". She was a true lady of Durham. Now I can tell you about Michael. In his retirement every morning he walked up the Bailey to Chad's, sat for half an hour or so talking to Bessie then he would go to Prebends' Bridge and return. Bessie was so loved by so many students. *(George Billingham)*

Michael Ramsey's Baptism, Childhood and Death through the eyes of those closest to him.

A notice on the font at St Andrew's Church, Horbling, Lincs
(courtesy of Mr Michael Barcroft)

"In 1977 Michael Ramsey, then Archbishop of Canterbury, visited Boston Parish Church in Lincolnshire to preach. After the service he asked to be taken to Horbling church on the edge of the Fens south of Sleaford, where his maternal grandfather had been vicar and where he had been baptised.

He shocked his companions by shuffling along to the font, walking round it and speaking to it, "Oh font, font, font; this is where my Christian life began."

This eccentric action spoke more loudly than any tome on the sacrament or architecture. Christianity is not at its core something to be believed in, but something to be lived, it changes our lives and the whole way we relate to each other. After that baptismal bath nothing can ever be the same. Ramsey knew that and he could smile and laugh at how strange the whole thing seemed."

Extracts from "Eighty Years and More, a Life Story by A. S. Ramsey" (Michael Ramsey's father)
(courtesy of Mr Michael Barcroft).

Michael, not yet five years old, had his little barrow and spade and used to work for hours side by side with the gardener, filling his barrow as the gardener did, wheeling it to the right spot and emptying it there.

Michael was much more normal in his attainments *[than his brother Frank, a brilliant mathematician—Editor]* with no gift for mathematics. Like Frank he went to Kings Choir School, Cambridge and then to Sandroyd, Wiltshire. In due course he tried for a scholarship at Winchester and was placed 13th in the roll. In an average year this would have secured a vacancy but for some reason associated with the call up of boys for military service there were only 12 vacancies that year, so he was rejected; but he won a scholarship at Repton, Derby and eventually came up to Magdalene, Oxford with a major scholarship.

Michael was a very difficult type of boy. He was always drawing and inattentive with a keen sense of the ludicrous and prone to laugh out loud whether it be in church, in form or parade. He had a good eye and might have been as good at games as Frank, had he been able to attend to the game, but he always seemed to be thinking about something else. He was not precocious in learning as Frank was but developed at a more normal pace. There was always a good deal of independence about his character and disposition.

Through staying with his uncle, AW Wilam, Organist of Ely Catheral, he acquired interest in and knowledge of the Cathedral buildings and sometimes surprised strangers by taking them round the Cathedral and telling them something of it history. In holiday times he cycled all round Cambridge visiting the village churches and making rubbings of brasses wherever he could find any. When the time came from him to go to Repton as a new boy he did not seem to mind the fact that neither his mother nor I were able to escort him and that he was the only new boy at his house to arrive without a parent in charge. Michael was keenly interested in politics and always a keen supporter of Asquith, and he was not deterred by any shyness from taking part in school debates. In fact, when as a new boy he saw armchairs at the front reserved for those who had spoken in a debate, he lost no time in acquiring the right to occupy one.

In September 1916 we took the family to a bungalow at Old Hunstanton Station for a few weeks and had our first experience of an air raid. About ten o-clock a Saturday night someone knocked on our window and shouted, "lights out". The children were all asleep in bed   Agnes and I stepped out to see what was happening. We could hear the throb of the engines of an aeroplane coming from the east over the sea. When the noise was coming vertically overhead it stopped and very soon a bomb fell and exploded half a mile away. Then seemed to be a trail of light with it just before it reached the ground.

Letters sent by Joan Ramsey describing Michael Ramsey's Death

ST JOHN'S HOME
St Mary's Road
Oxford OX4 1QE

tel. (0865) 722497

May, 1988

My dear Denis & Val

It was lovely to have your message. Thank you very much. Remembering and looking forward in love and peace as Michael did, I am both happy and helped by your remembrance.

Michael was spared the weary illness expected by the doctor – & just died very happily & peacefully in his own bed with the Rev. Mother to help us. It was lovely to see such peace in his smile & also delight! Thankyou for years & years of being friends – which I'm sure will go on!

With love to you all

Joan

Courtesy of Denis and Val Trigg

May, 1988

My dear Maurice

It was lovely to have your message. Thank you very much. Remembering and looking forward in love and peace as Michael did, I am both happy and helped by your remembrance. I remember you both in Durham days & I loved going there for the Memorial service last week & now I am off to the one in York — but one doesn't get a chance to talk to everyone so send this to make sure I tell you how I loved your letter. I never saw

Michael more serene & radiantly happy than when he died. I'm sure he was seeing the Glory he often talked about, even more wonderful than he'd known it could be — So that is very comforting as we plod on. Greetings to you both.   Joan Ramsey

Courtesy of the Revd Canon Maurice Simmons

155